"From a passionate father's heart to encourage and equip his daughter to love and pursue writing, we have *Letters from the Mountain*. In the interest of full disclosure, though, the lessons are for all writers, young and old, and in reality, not just for writers but for each of us who daily go out into the world to write our own stories as living epistles. While the book addresses the essence of writing, the wisdom and insights Palpant communicates in his lessons are universal. As an "old" writer, I was blessed and inspired to keep climbing my mountain and to leave some trail markers along the way for others to follow. I wish I had this book thirty years ago. I love it."

—Cynthia Heald, author of *Becoming a Woman of Simplicity*

"Writing is a form of communication but it ultimately seeks to become a form of communion—between hearts and minds and between the generations. If you seek a wise and generous guide to how communication—through love, prayer, and the mastery of craft—can grow into communion, *Letters from the Mountain* is a wonderful place to start."

—Gregory Wolfe, author of *Beauty Will Save the World*

"This book is a beautiful work of grace, bound by love and fueled by art, a blessing in every sense to the reader. I enjoyed every word."

—Jeff Goins, author of *The Art of Work*

"In the beautiful epistolary tradition evocative of Rilke, Ben Palpant examines what it means to be an attentive writer of faith, and to pass the creative commending of God's mighty works to a future generation."

—Carolyn Weber, author of *Surprised by Oxford*

"Sometimes you can read just one sentence and know that the writer has a gift. Ben Palpant is one of those people. This book on writing, framed as a series of letters to his daughter, is a window into his big, generous, and pastoral soul. There's a lot of wisdom here, and I'm grateful for the way Palpant is using his gift to give it away."

—Andrew Peterson, singer/songwriter, author of *The Wingfeather Saga*

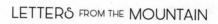
LETTERS FROM THE MOUNTAIN

OTHER BOOKS by BEN PALPANT

POETRY
Sojourner Songs
The Stranger: Meditations on the Christ

NON-FICTION
A Small Cup of Light
Honey from the Lion's Mouth

CHILDREN'S STORIES
Pepin and the Magician

LETTERS
FROM THE
MOUNTAIN

BEN PALPANT

RABBIT ROOM
— PRESS —

Published by
RABBIT ROOM PRESS
3321 Stephens Hill Lane
Nashille, Tennessee 37013
info@rabbitroom.com

Unless otherwise indicated, Scripture quotations are from The Holy Bible, New King James Version, Copyright 1982 by Thomas Nelson, Inc.
Used by permission. All rights reserved.

Extract from "The Singing Bowl" from *The Singing Bowl* by Malcolm Guite,
© Malcolm Guite 2013. Published by Canterbury Press.
Used by permission. All rights reserved.

ISBN 9781951872076

Printed in the United States of America

Book Design by Ben Palpant
Cover Design by Ben Palpant

To Kialynn
a "catching of happiness"
—Philip Larkin

"Whatever I tell you in the dark, speak in the light; and what you hear in the ear, preach on the housetops."

—Matthew 10:27

"My entire soul is a cry, and all my work the commentary on that cry."

—Nikos Kazantzakis,
Report to Greco

"You'll be bothered from time to time by storms, fog, snow. When you are, think of those who went through it before you, and say to yourself, 'What they could do, I can do.'"

—Antoine de Saint-Exupery,
Wind, Sand and Stars

TABLE OF CONTENTS

FOREWORD

"Things aren't all so tangible and sayable as people would usually have us believe; most experiences are unsayable, they happen in a space that no word has ever entered, and more unsayable than all other things are works of art, those mysterious existences, whose life endures beside our own small, transitory life."
—Rainer Maria Rilke, from *Letters to a Young Poet*

The book you hold is, in its most basic form, a collection of letters from father to daughter, a collection grown out of the largely unsayable experiences and mysterious existences that are my relationship with my dad.

As the title suggests, our relationship has been much like climbing a mountain, my dad up above on the trail, marking the rougher parts of the road, sometimes holding my hand, and sometimes passing down advice.

When I was twelve, I hiked several miles down a mountain stream with my dad and little sister. When we were too footsore

and fatigued to keep going, Dad decided it would be just as difficult to walk back the way we came as to cut up the high bank
two hundred feet to the road. The former was too far. He chose
the latter, praying that it would not prove too steep. We crossed
the river, my sister and I, grasping my dad's hand as he stepped
over the stones and the water, which I remember rushing toward
us foaming and angry. We reached the other side wet, my dad
wearing only a single shoe, and my sister wide-eyed and terrified.

When we tried to climb out of the ravine, the sand of the
bank fell through our hands, hot and dry. My sister and I could
do nothing but picture our car up on the road, past the heat and
the dirt and the pine needles that had slipped into our shorts.
I remember climbing up the bank just behind my dad, trying
to follow his movements and the footprints he left behind. I
remember grabbing onto a newly-rooted pine sapling and
feeling it loosen its hold in the ground, leaving me dangling
and unbalanced with nothing but my toes in the crumbling wall
and my dad's hand to keep me steady.

I could see the edge when I looked up—the place where the
side of the ravine leveled off—and I remember my dad encouraging us to keep our eyes fixed on it. Too terrified by the height
to do much otherwise, my sister and I did our best, only to reach
it and realize the ledge we had looked toward marked only an
indent in the hill before it shot up even higher and steeper. In
the moment, Dad appeared determined and undaunted, but he
later admitted feeling terrified that one or both of his girls might
slip and fall from what proved to be nearly a vertical climb.

When we finally reached the top and felt the road under our feet, Dad hugged us both and told us we were brave. Then we walked to the car and ate cantaloupe until our sides hurt, our hands dripping with melon juice.

My whole life has been like that ravine, and I'm still climbing it. I feel unbalanced most of the time, and I find I'm always looking up toward my father with his hand outstretched—I climb eagerly after him, anticipating a word, a hug, and a kindness that will make my sides hurt and my hands drip with gratuitous generosity.

A large part of this climb with my dad has been through art, and his stories have become some of the most concrete anchors on the side of this mountain. The first were bedtime stories about a little girl named Eliak, who managed to fall through sandboxes into castles and found magical things in the mirrors at the end of the hall. Later, it was my dad reading *Grimm's Fairy Tales* aloud at night, haunting my mind with beautiful and mysterious woods. After that came an avalanche of children's stories, memories of reading the books from his shelf after bedtime by the light of a cracked door, and then the books he began to write and edit and publish. Each gave me another handhold as I watched the footprints he left behind and tried to copy his movements.

This book is a record of the wisdom he's collected over the course of his climb, whether from art, stories, the Christian life, or simply the everyday challenges of the mountain. I'm told these letters were based off of *Letters to a Young Poet* by Rainer

Maria Rilke, who gave similar advice to an aspiring young writer. Rilke tried to put words to the unsayable experiences and mysterious existences that we all discover in life. My father has tried to do the same—to speak to another climber on the journey, to give advice, and to give a hand-up along the way. In this, he speaks not only to me, climbing in his shadow, but also to everyone who picks up this book—writer, reader, Christian, or otherwise. After all, we're climbing this mountain together, and we would do well to take the hand of one who has gone before us.

Oxford, 2018
Kialynn Palpant

THE MOUNTAIN BECKONS

Dear One,

The soft rain falling outside my window will soon wash away all traces of winter. I can smell inevitable spring in the air. You love winter snow, but you also love the rain and perhaps the falling rain has me thinking of you as I do tonight.

I imagine you leaning over your studies long after the sun has dropped behind the cityscape that spreads out from your small apartment, or feverishly pounding the keys in hopes that something you make—a story or a poem—will one day mean something special to someone else. I imagine you staring out the window for a moment to watch the city lights flicker on.

And suddenly you're with me again, wearing pigtails and clasping my hand. We're standing at the base of a majestic mountain. The footpath lies narrow and relatively flat here in front of us, but it begins to wind up the mountain where the pines thicken. We both know that if we take this path, the difficulties ahead will tax our endurance. But when we lift our gaze, the mountain peak glimmers above the pines and cloud cover. Beauty calls. Mystery beckons. We're coming.

But I'm only dreaming.

The freckled girl from my memory is now a woman, far from the fire in my grate. I sit alone in a mountain shack and listen to the rain on the roof, watch it slide down the glass. I hug a wool sweater to my shoulders. She climbs the trail somewhere far below in the dense woods. I cannot see her. I cannot clasp her hand. But perhaps these letters will show her the way when she loses the path. Perhaps she will read them and hear my familiar voice and know that I am somewhere ahead, expectant.

But I'm only dreaming.

I'm seated at my desk, trying to learn love's language and its cadence—choosing what to write, where to warn and where to give hope, when to say "I nearly died at that mile marker" or "I lost my way just ahead there" or "Keep climbing! The view from here is stunning!" or how to say, "My heart waits on the side of this mountain—waits for you, little one."

So I begin again.

Dear One, a father desires to share some of his hard-earned convictions and half-formed ideas with his daughter, whom he hopes will come to terms with her gifting and calling. He longs for her faith journey to culminate at the peak where the

360-degree view will undo her, where she will weep for sheer joy, where she will laugh with exhilaration.

The principles essential to his own writing journey have proven mysterious, paradoxical, and bewildering even after all these years. He would prefer a less difficult trail. He would prefer a white chalk line marking the easiest ascent up the mountain. But this path is not like that. This mountain is not conducive to ease. Day hikers never last long here.

A father would also like his advice to be firm like granite. Sure-footed. He comes from a long line of opinionated people—French, German, and Swede—and must reckon with their blood in his veins. They were not always correct. And sometimes he is wrong, too. Nevertheless, his advice is not his alone. He accumulated it by experience and from those who climbed before him. They left their travel journals for his aid. They left markers where the trail vanished in the underbrush or along the broken slate.

And it troubles him that no single letter, or book of letters, could ever say all that needs to be said about this writing journey. He must come to terms with this limitation and his daughter knows that her father has never accepted such things lying down.

Nevertheless, he has limited his advice to those areas at which personal cultivation and cultural cultivation converge—where to expect pitfalls, how to develop essential habits, when to stay anchored. Every word he writes carries undying love. Each suggestion is intended as a gesture of kindness, like a good cup of tea in the morning to help her wake into the light of this thing called life. They are intended to clear a path for her in this sprawling, difficult terrain—to focus her vision, to light the way, to propel her gently where she might go.

This life is a long one for writers who reach three score and ten. It is even longer for others. An equal measure of persistence and patience is necessary. Persistence through natural resistance. Patience with yourself, with ideas, with interruptions, with inspirations. Carrying a single project to completion can be frustratingly slow, but the race "is not to the swift nor the battle to the strong" (Ecc. 9:11).

Life is a gradual dawning on the heart and mind. A few "Eureka!" moments might punctuate a life, but most of the time we travel in relative obscurity, doing our best. Not until we crest a ridge line do we look back and say, "Ah, I see! Now I understand." And when we turn forward again, another ascent waits.

These letters are my attempt to reach out over the miles and clasp your hand as you climb. To whisper encouragement in your ear as I did when you were young. To spur you on toward love and good works. To remember our story. To lean my forehead against yours and give you my blessing: from the humble to the humble, to the glory of God. Amen.

THE WRITING LIFE

"For even the Son of Man did not come to be served, but to serve, and to give His life a ransom for many."
—Mark 10:45

One day we drove the van as usual, and the next day it died. Just like that, it was unfixable. The timing could not have been worse. America was staggering under a financial crisis and our family of seven felt it keenly. My teacher's income afforded us little margin already. This unexpected need crippled my optimism. Your mother and I closed the bedroom door and whispered our urgent prayer: "O Lord, provide."

We had been in there for a long time, praying and problem solving, when we heard a soft knock on the door. I opened the door to see you—all pigtails and freckles—smiling. You clutched something behind your back.

"I know our van is broken," you said. "And I know we have no money. And I heard you crying. And I know you're praying.

So the kids and I agreed we'd like to help."

You flushed with excitement and put out your little hands. They held a jar of crumpled dollar bills and a few coins. "We put our savings together and it adds up to thirty-three dollars and fifty-seven cents. Maybe you can use this to buy a car."

Your generosity forcefully, unforgettably intruded on our grief. I knew how long you had worked to save that money. I knew how hard it was for you to convince your little brother and sisters to give up their savings, too. You weren't trying to be pious. You weren't trying to gain leverage. You weren't hoping to get anything in return. I knew that what I held in my hands constituted your everything. Pure generosity.

In that moment, you embodied the very nature of God. It is his nature to *give*. Generously. Unpretentiously. Continuously. To give everything with no expectation of return.

GENERATIVITY

You're a writer. Here, at the outset of your life, embrace the call to imitate God, to give everything. Nothing aligns closer to God's heart than self-sacrifice and generous service (Matt. 7:7-11, Rom. 8:32). And would you really want it any other way? It has become your nature. For some people, life is an endless pleasure hunt. For others it's simply a pursuit of glory. For writers like you, life boils down to nothing less than giving yourself away.

When I call you a writer, I do not use the term casually. Something about the word "writer" is very personal. I've never met a writer who felt otherwise. I've met bankers who could wear the title, "banker," or take it off as they wished. The same for mechanics and pilots, but writers feel differently, as if it's part of who they are. The term comprises the entire individual. Like a man and his personality, the two are inseparable. They are one and the same thing. Neither can you divide a writer from her identity as one.

The term "writer" denotes continuous action: writers feel compelled to write, think about writing, and find every opportunity to write. All of life's experiences equip, propel, and inspire them in that pursuit. In other words, "writer" describes more than the work they do. It describes the heart's inclination, the mind's purpose, and the spirit's direction. When you realize the world's desperate need for your work, these drives will only increase.

The world is full of spiritually-starved people. Hold their hands, look into their eyes, and listen to the words behind their words. You will hear a silent, universal plea, *Care for me, friend. Give me a cup of cool water. Feed me with words refashioned, renewed, and flung into this city of dying lights.* And how can you perform this generous task if all of your life—resting, laughing, working, praying, eating, and writing—is not aimed outward, toward Christ and toward others? When you write, keep your audience in mind without caving to vanity. You're not writing to be adored, you're writing to serve.

We know many kinds of Christians on this faith journey. Some aim to get. Others aim to give. For most of us, our aims vacillate between the two. One day finds us selfishly grabbing and the next day finds us generous again. Perhaps this is what it means to be human rather than divine. Even in God's house on a Sunday morning, sitting beneath arching beams, my heart cannot decide between selflessness and selfishness.

And then I glance across the pews and see my friends—beloved children of God—emanating hope, redemption, insight, and transcendence. They pray when I'm unable, listen when I'm distracted, sing in my stead. They inspire a God-hunger in me, compelling me to do something meaningful with my life. What word can I use to describe their multiplying effect on others? Perhaps *generative* is that word.

We inherited the word from the Latin *generare*, meaning "beget" or "generate." "Generative" is an adjective with broad application, but it certainly applies to the arts. Generative artists *beget* new ideas, new visions, different life choices in us, they ignite further creativity. You have tasted this generativity before. Remember that song you once heard that made you want to write a poem? Remember that story you read that inspired you to write your own stories? Beautiful and compelling works beget something new in us.

Many artists accidentally generate creativity in others, but those who want their work to last are more intentional. You can be like them, embodying the biblical charge to live focused on others, doing nothing out of selfish ambition (Phil. 2:3). Your investment in people will generate energy in others, inspiring new ideas, new visions, new life choices.

If you would be like them, write in the following three ways. First, aim to enrich the future—not just the present. Second, work hard to inspire spiritual depth in others. And third, give everything—including time and energy—to serve others. In other words, be intentional. Cultivate the world generationally, inspirationally, and generously.

GENERATIONAL GENERATIVITY

From time to time, we all have difficulty looking beyond the end of a work day. Focused on our small circle of influence, burdened under tiny demands, and impatient to do what we want to do, we lack the perspective necessary for important work. But generative work is important and, therefore, demands a generational vision.

Generative writers recognize that cultural vitality depends upon an eternal perspective in which individuals work and create for all generations and for all peoples. Age, gender, race, geography, and even religion are no barrier to the generative writer's effectiveness. For example, Shel Silverstein's *The Giving Tree*, C. S. Lewis's *The Lion, the Witch and the Wardrobe*, and Alexandre Dumas's *The Count of Monte Cristo* (one of your favorites) cross every barrier. Their work endures because it is timeless and treasured. Like your grandmother's quilts that warm anyone who crawls beneath them, generative writing warms anyone who reads it. No matter the generational difference or distance, we are inspired.

INSPIRATIONAL GENERATIVITY

Generative writers transfix the heart and mind. Their work enthralls. We feel transported to a higher vantage point on the mountain. Because they have transmuted their personal experience into inspiration or encouragement for others, their vulnerability and clarity invite us into a shared experience that eclipses our own. The epiphanies born from their sufferings and joys spark spiritual insights and spur us to action. Like a silkworm, they produce strong, durable, and beautiful work from their depths.

Their work changes us, startles us, invites us. We feel keenly aware of their kindred spirit. In this darkened wilderness of existence, they open our eyes to see that we're not alone. It seems to us that someone has struck a match to light a lamp, revealing beauty, mystery, and hope. Now the soul is irrevocably illumined, charged. Now the soul is hurtled into the unknown, sent on a different trajectory toward majestic mountain peaks. This radiance, transcendence, and kinship differentiates generative writers from all others.

GENEROUS GENERATIVITY

And here is another essential difference: most of us bemoan our limitations of time and energy, but generative writers do not. Or, not enough to prevent them from plugging away. They recognize a deep cultural need that can only be met by sacrificial generosity. While some people find every cause to shield time and conserve energy, to safeguard their heart and hoard their ideas, generative people lavishly give them away.

Generosity is the bone marrow of the generative life, reflecting the truth found in 2 Corinthians 9:6 that "He who sows sparingly will also reap sparingly, and he who sows bountifully will also reap bountifully." Paul exhorts the Corinthians to live lives of radical generosity, contending that those saved by grace will be promiscuous with their material goods and their immaterial gifts. He preached a generous God, able to bless abundantly, so that in all things at all times, having all that we need, we can abound in every good work (2 Cor. 9:8).

You will soon discover that misers of time, attention, opportunity, reputation, energy, labor, and money cannot live generatively—their cultural impact is usually small. You will also discover that the biblical call to give has familial, societal, and global impact. Those who give their lives away are culture makers.

Who is surprised by this revelation? Did not Christ lead by example? At every point in the gospels, Jesus lavishly flings his life away. Christ fed so we can feed. He served so we can serve. He laid his life down so that we might lay ours down. Christ broke bread and gave thanks so that we might do the same.

I've known the most ordinary, poorest of the poor, who, having experienced God's gratuitous gifting, showed remarkable generosity themselves. They did not dwell on their limitations or lack. They embraced the generous life. Regular people who give away themselves—not just their finances—can have remarkable impact. As the scriptures illustrate, unspectacular people can make a spectacular difference.

GENERATIVITY IN THE BIBLE

The scriptures teem with generative people—Joseph, Hosea, John the Baptist, Mary Magdalene—but one nameless character exemplifies it best. The peasant boy with his five rolls and two fish in Luke 9 offered everything. He didn't have much, he didn't know whom God would feed, and he didn't know how God would do it, but he gave anyway. One forgettable boy whose one small act had a ripple effect. He is our role model.

His story shows us that ordinariness is extraordinary. And nature shows likewise. Look at an ordinary wheat field. Ten million heads of wheat wave in the wind. Each head waits to be harvested so that it can give away twenty-two kernels of wheat. By an amazing process, those two-hundred and twenty million kernels are changed into flour and used by a girl somewhere to bake cupcakes for her ten friends. Or one ordinary stone tossed into a pond creates one hundred ripples, wave upon wave.

Each of us is like a head of wheat or like a stone. Harvest us, toss us, watch us impact our surroundings. We may not feel adequately talented, confident, insightful, or brave enough to serve others, but we get to give everything we have anyway. Recognize your economic, intellectual, geographical, social, and skill restrictions, then learn to live and give freely within those limitations. Wait in faith for God to multiply and surprise.

How kind of Jesus to perform a miracle with a little boy's simple offering. Here is proof of God's multiplying power. If God can use that boy's few loaves and fishes, then you need not burden yourself with high and mighty holiness or tasks too great for you. If you have a proper mindset, then your circumstances, your relationships, your health, and your geography are somehow advantageous to you, not a barrier to your success.

David, the shepherd boy, had limitations too. Undersized, poor, and uneducated, he had every reason to cower before Goliath or to posture before Saul or to go off and play stickball when he faced defeat. He did not. He used what God gave him in faithful service to God. Better to be David with his sling, natural and fitted to his experience and size, than to be David trying to fight in Saul's armor.

God has specially equipped you and placed you to meet the needs of those around you in meaningful and lasting ways. God likes to perform miracles by using your life—with all of its constraints and foibles—to impact a soul not your own. When that happens, rejoice and stand in awe before a God who multiplied your loaves and fishes. He will use your life in more ways than you imagine.

A GENERATIVE VOICE FOR THE VOICELESS

I once wrote a memorial for a man whom I dearly loved. In my opinion, the piece did not adequately describe his wonderful life nor my deep affection, so the sheer number of people who thanked me for putting into words the pain and hope and love that they could not express surprised me. What a sobering experience. Unbeknownst to me, I became their mouthpiece. I had written the memorial out of my own love and grief, but others could now say, "Yes, that's how I feel. That's what I wanted to say!" We do our best, you see, and God multiplies the work. He uses our sincere, selfless acts to serve and nourish many lives besides our own.

People hunger for writers who can speak for them and to them in beautiful and compelling ways. Although we live in a literate society, our literacy is largely functional. We do not read widely, nor deeply, nor much, and we find ourselves often bereft of the right words. Ironically, the problem is exacerbated by the sheer volume of words that barrage us from all sides: songs, social networks, advertisements, Twitter feeds, blog posts, texts, news updates, and celebrity reports stagger the soul. The words lack meaning. People don't feel spoken to or spoken for.

I met a woman the other day so inundated by words that she has forsworn them. She does not read blogs. She does not listen to podcasts. She wants nothing but quiet. What she needs, what we all need, is not writers who can generate more volume, but writers who offer the right word at the right time. We need writers who aim for the soul, writers who speak to us and for us—generative writers.

THE WORLD HUNGERS

What the world fails to give so many people—faith, dignity, transcendence, hope, love, and restoration—you can give to them in your life and in your writing. They want to know that they are not nameless in the cosmic scheme of things, that their stories are not meaningless. I'm reminded of that poignant scene in *Till We Have Faces* where the city's people gather at Psyche's gate. As she walks among them, touching and healing along the way, the crowd grows silent in response to the moment's beauty. Jesus moved among the people similarly. How quickly we forget that Christ's missional work to bring life took place in a society glutted on death and power. Our society, like his, throbs with real people whose hearts and minds matter to God, but who are neck deep in relational rivalries, religious pluralism, identity crises, and lust. These perennial problems are inherited from our first parents whose fall in Genesis continues to manifest itself in crooked cultures built by crooked hearts. A casual observation of our songs, our amusements, our wars, and our work reveals a spiritually starved people who need nourishment only God can provide. Writers like you can be God's hands, offering soul food to the world.

Listen, dearest, a vast and voiceless throng longing for clarity and kindness and justice gathers outside your door. They huddle together in the cold and await your words—hold nothing from them. Give to them your gifts, your time, your comfort, your stories, your life. Give them what God has given you.

Give through writing what God has given you

Our goal to meet the world's needs—to serve generationally, inspirationally, and generously—is lofty, but attainable. It propels us forward. It directs our intentions. This goal can be met using any genre you prefer—fiction, poetry, research articles, essays, blog posts. Each genre speaks to readers differently. Each is uniquely suited to move the heart and inform the mind.

FESTINA LENTE

But we do not become generative writers overnight. Our skills and insights do not arrive fully formed. The writing life is an evolving one, moving at the pace of our experiences and growth. Learn from your experiences, grow from them, refine your life. Write, rewrite, and refine your work. It is a painstaking and gradual process without immediate reward. Embrace the process. Work like those faithful people in the book of Nehemiah who steadily built, one day at at time. Every kind of person helped build the wall, even a man and his daughters (Neh. 3:12) and two men who could only help with the portion of the wall just outside their front door (Neh. 3:23).

As you learn to be a writer, carry the paradox called 'patient urgency.' The old adage, *festina lente*, is still a worthy one. Writing is, indeed, an act that requires practice and experience, just like a chef in the kitchen who must work several pots at once, each at a different temperature and each requiring attention at the right time and in due proportion. *Festina lente*. Keep learning, keep laboring, keep listening. *Festina lente*.

We can only do what we can with what we have in the time allotted to us. Let us keep our eyes fixed firmly on this mountain's summit, remembering all the while to trust the Author and Finisher of our faith who will complete his work in us. This entire generative life is an act of faith in the God who equipped us to write and will see to it that he uses us according to his desires. Let us tuck that promise into our heart's pocket and remind each other of it.

THE GENERATIVE LIFE MOTTO

The Christian life is not simply a moral pursuit—a call to kindness or purity—it subsumes those small purposes within a larger purpose of generativity. We're Christ's hands and feet—continuing his sacrificial, priestly, and kingly work—laboring with the Holy Spirit to cultivate hearts and minds into the likeness of Jesus Christ—starting with our own. Christ came to renew our humanity, so the Christian understands that the biblical view of liberation and humanization includes all people. We get to be a part of that. We get to humanize and invite others into a more human life under the open sky of God's grace. Christians waste a lot of energy trying to impact culture rather than investing in people who create culture. Such labor requires that generative writers be patient in their perspective, intentional in their work, and charged by a transcendent vision. We need the Holy Spirit to grant us strength, wisdom, hope, and encouragement. He is the source of our vitality and effectiveness. We're his messengers. He amplifies our voice and multiplies our efforts.

Ecclesiastes 11:1 says, "Cast your bread upon the waters, For you will find it after many days." It's an enigmatic but essential verse for generative living. Regardless of the many interpretations, the principle of the verse remains the same: give generously and you will find it multiplied and returned to you— bless widely and you will be blessed.

A river flows through the center of your heart's castle and out into the city of man. Set your little bread—be it a word or an idea—upon the water and let it follow the current. Someone downstream will pick it up and take it home and be fed by it.

BENEDICTION

May the God who made you, equipped you, and placed you give you patience to climb this mountain of life. May he use your gifts—meager as they may feel—to generate further creativity in others. May your daily aim be generational, inspirational, and generous.

THE SANCTIFIED IMAGINATION

"The hardest thing of all to see is what is really there."
—J. A. Baker, *The Peregrine*

My best friend lived on a small river. The path from his back deck to the river wound downhill, through tall grasses, and beneath drooping willow trees until it terminated at a sandy strand on the river's edge. The water slowed at a bend, creating a deep swimming hole. Only the brave ventured into those dark waters. I rarely did.

One day, a Vietnamese exchange student visited my friend's family. We introduced him to the swimming hole and to the delights of sand-castle building along the shore. The three of us had worked for some time on a castle when he put his finger to his lips and peeked over his shoulder. While I watched, he performed a back flip into the shallow water of the river and came up with a trout wriggling in his hands.

His acrobatic dexterity verged on magic to my young mind. I wondered if he had eyes in the back of his head. But the truth of the matter is that he was simply more observant and more dexterous than me. He had obviously practiced attentiveness and precision for a long time. Like that boy, Christians can practice a spiritual attentiveness, learning to see what others overlook—to perceive behind, beneath, and beyond the senses. They can learn to use the soul's vision.

IMAGINATION DEFINED

Some have called the imagination the eye of the soul. It interprets and weaves together received stimuli to form a coherent whole, a story. A robust imagination recognizes meaning and coherence behind the apparent randomness and chaos of life. One of the most important goals for Christian living, therefore, is to align our imagination with God's vision and work, matching our narratives with his.

LEARN TO SEE

Christians believe that all material things point to ultimate things, the seen pointing to the unseen. We believe that the universe was created as one seamless fabric, with every created thing participating well or poorly in a meaningful, divine dance. Like Isaiah and Jacob, we're learning to match what we see with what we believe, learning to see the visible as a container for the

*The way you imagine the world dictates how they live and what they make. *how you live, what you make*

invisible, the whole earth full of God's glory (Isa. 6:3), every inch of matter infused with his splendor.

Gerard Manley Hopkins called this world, "the news of God." Generative writers pay attention to that news. They know that the way people imagine the world dictates how they live and what they make. If their imagination aligns with God's vision, their work may unveil God's intimate presence and activity. In that case, their writing will restore, recalibrate, and realign the imaginations of others who read it.

In my climb up the mountain of faith, I've come to believe that the Christian experience ultimately comes down to developing eyes that see as God sees—or, more accurately, learning to see God's activity through God's eyes. As Simone Weil poignantly said, the Christian religion is nothing less than a looking. Many Christians spend their best effort on trying to be holy or on doing good deeds, and they forget to see.

PRACTICE A CHRISTOCENTRIC CONSCIOUSNESS *great analogy*

When I was a boy, cereal boxes sometimes came with surprises inside. One morning, my siblings and I opened the box to find a paper written with line upon line of random letters. We could make no sense of those lines without the decoding device, which we found at the bottom of the box and which told us to only count every third letter. When we wrote down every third letter, understandable words and phrases appeared where we previously saw only gibberish. It's a simplistic comparison to make, but Jesus is like that decoding device. His birth, life, death, resurrection, and continued activity in the world unlock the mysteries hidden in God. So many things in the world, in God's word, in our own lives, seem to make little sense upon first glance, but Jesus can help make sense of them.

For this reason, the medieval theologians practiced what Luci Shaw calls a Christocentric consciousness. They watched for ways in which everything pointed to Christ. They saw layers of meaning in Scripture and in the world: the *literal* layer, the *allegorical* layer, the *tropological* or moral layer, and the *anagogic* layer.

It works this way: On a literal level, a visible thing is a visible thing (like a rock). On an allegorical level, that visible thing might point to another visible thing (a rock is like Christ). On a moral level, that visible thing might indicate the right thing to be done (since Christ is strong and stable, we should build our lives upon him like we would build upon a rock) and the anagogical level leads us from the visible thing into a picture of the invisible, divine life where we participate with heaven (building upon Christ into and through eternity).

No matter the terrain or the weather along faith's journey, generative Christians have a wonderful opportunity to stay captivated by the light of Christ, to stare into the Son and then to see all things and all people colored by that light. Indeed, when the soul's eye is fixed on Jesus, it sees him everywhere. That is to say, what seizes the imagination impacts absolutely every-thing—what we love, what we think, what we do.

NEWNESS
seeing the world
redeemed *Letters from the Mountain* | 23

For this very reason, Christ came to transform our imaginations, to change the way we see everything. He gives each of his elect a new heart, new mind, new eyes, new ears, new hands, new feet. He initiates new passions, new lines of thought, renewed spiritual sight, new depth of hearing, new things to do, and a new life trajectory. You get to enflesh that newness with your words. You get to hold fast to the truth found in God's Word that makes all things new.

Many writers dream dreams and cast visions. Unless those dreams and visions are in concord with God's Word, such writers are prophets of the deceit of their own heart (Jer. 23:26). So long as you remain anchored in God's truth, your dreams and visions will continue God's work of making all things new. You will build what God builds, break what he breaks, divide what he divides, and cultivate what he cultivates. Your work will mean more and last longer.

THE SACRAMENTS TEACH US TO SEE

Even at the first communion, Christ was training his disciples in this sanctified imagination when he said to look, touch, taste, and digest. This physical meal loaded now with metaphor was the ultimate renewing of their minds (Rom. 12:2), giving fresh life and vigor to the way they saw the world, but also shifting the direction of their lives from self-focused to God-focused. When Jesus told his disciples to see him in that bread and that wine on the table, he forever changed the way they saw all bread and all wine. Each time they ate and drank—no matter the circumstances—they would remember that moment. They would remember him. They were given eyes of faith, and ordinary objects were suddenly infused with divine significance.

Christians learn from an early age to see through the Sacraments—bread, wine, water—to the reality they represent. While the Sacraments are a means of grace, a sacramental attunement is a spiritual attentiveness to the way all bread, all wine, all water now points back to the divine.

One of the most beautiful and meaningful things that Christ did was to take bread between his hands and tear it, offering it to his disciples as a memorial of his upcoming work on the cross. And after his resurrection, when he broke the bread again in Emmaus and then vanished, he gave his friends—who were never the same—one more reason to see ordinary objects differently. In so much as he did it for them, he has done it for us.

Imagine sitting with Jesus and his friends at that rickety wooden table in that small, unremarkable house. Oh the ecstasy, the sudden epiphany! He took the ordinary and made it extraordinary, as God intended at creation, reshaping in their and our imaginations all such simple acts like eating, drinking, and bathing. These activities are not the Sacraments themselves, but they remind us of great spiritual things and invest life with a million markers of the divine. The sanctified imagination is sacramentally attuned to those markers.

Even bathing takes on a new significance. It points to baptism, to a larger reality of cleansing and identity. It points to Christ, who washed his friends' feet. I have, over the years, periodically washed your feet along with your siblings' in an effort to imitate Jesus in his servant leadership.

The exercise reminds me of my calling—which I often fail to fulfill—but it also reminds you of yours. When I fill an ordinary plastic tub with ordinary water, set it on an ordinary towel, and invite my ordinary child to sit on an ordinary chair, I infuse the ordinary with the extraordinary in imitation of Jesus.

When I dip my child's little feet in the water and rub them with my thumbs, I whisper these words: "I love you. I've always loved you. I will love you forever. I promise to serve you and love you all of my life. I wash your feet to remind you of Jesus, and this is how I want you to serve your mother, your siblings, and all those people God puts into your life." It is my hope that when you see that plastic tub leaning in the bathroom, you will remember the times I washed your feet. When you remember those foot washings, you will remember Christ who didn't think twice about emptying himself and becoming a servant of all.

Generative writers do the equivalent of foot washing, but on a larger scale. They serve their readers, awakening them to the extraordinary in the ordinary, the meaningful in the apparently meaningless. Their work says, "Look! Do you see the hand of God? Listen! Can you hear his quiet whisper?" Everything they write says, "Do you feel the earth shudder? That is God walking. Do you hear the skylark whistle? That is God singing."

Some poor souls imagine that this world is empty of ultimate meaning. They believe that what we do is nothing but the blind reflex of an animalistic biology. They suggest that our stories and songs are only the heart's futile cries in the sandstorm of human suffering.

Christians, however, believe that the universe surges with meaning in the same way that a Texas oil field burgeons with oil. What looks like a dry, unremarkable wilderness hides incredible value. This view of the world deepens and enriches the generative life and writing. Nurture this view of the world for your heart's sake and for the sake of all those people you will someday serve.

LOVE YOUR LITTLE POSTAGE STAMP OF NATIVE SOIL

To writers—at least the best of us—there is no impoverished person, place, or thing. All of life offers endless inspiration. Your experiences give your writing a unique tone and texture. You will discover, like William Faulkner, that even your own "little postage stamp of native soil" is worth exploring and enjoying. Every house, for example, is a cradle for the imagination (Gaston Bachelard, *The Poetics of Space*).

Ray Bradbury had a small journal in which he recorded noun after noun from his childhood: matchbook, stove, sandbox, scissors. Hundreds of these rather regular items filled his journal. In his memory, he would visually walk through locations—his grandmother's house, the apartment, the backwoods—to find more of these items. Each item represented a story or a feeling from his life. These became the source of his creativity. His wonderful short stories usually started with some small object from his experience.

Let your childhood spaces—the playhouse, the back forty, the pond where small birds dipped on hot days, and the secret door between your room and your sister's—serve as the birthplace of your inspiration and work. From your ordinary childhood, you will glean so many lessons, metaphors, perspectives, story starts, anecdotes, and ideas. God sees your ordinary life and knows that it is still remarkable. He has given all of it to you as a gift.

CULTIVATE YOUR LITTLE POSTAGE STAMP OF NATIVE SOIL

Not only is your little postage stamp of native soil a meaningful place and a source of inspiration, it's also a place worth cultivating. God's eyes are gardener's eyes. When you see life with his eyes, you'll see that, like a garden, life brims with potential. It takes a special hopefulness and resilience combined with vision and wisdom to cultivate our existence effectively. You are called to that lofty work.

I recently spoke to a friend of mine who visited Nepal and was astonished to find rural farmers growing potatoes and rice at an altitude of 4,000 feet. His astonishment was doubled by the fact that the fields were cut out of the steep mountainsides. Where seasonal monsoons used to rush down the mountain, carrying all the soil with them, terraced fields now harnessed all that water to irrigate their rice and potato fields.

Anyone visiting those mountains two-hundred years ago would have seen nothing but a recipe for disaster: steep hillsides, heavy rainfall, and lots of mud ready to slide. But someone came along who understood agricultural engineering and careful cultivation—some nameless nobody—and changed that region of Nepal for the better. Metaphorically speaking, that could be you. It takes no genius to see that many of our infrastructures are eroding. Apart from God and the faithful labor of those serving alongside him, who can stop these societal mud slides? Who can help prevent erosion in the lives of those you know and meet? You can.

Agricultural engineering and cultivation is a Christian calling in the world, and the same is true of writing. Writers get to terrace and cultivate the unplantable land. We get to embody beauty, truth, and moral goodness where the world experiences only mud slides. We get to not only hold off erosion, we get to replace the erosion with gardens. It is work that participates in God's redemptive work here in our little postage stamp of native soil.

PRACTICE OMNIVOROUS ATTENTIVENESS

Learning to see this life as it is—loaded with divine meaningfulness and potential—quickens your spiritual pulse and awakens you to the uniqueness of everything and everyone around you. It opens your eyes to the sensory details that distinguish one place from another, one moment from a million others, but only if you stay awake. Only if you practice seeing.

That's one reason why Alan Jacobs praised C. S. Lewis and called us to imitate his "omnivorous attentiveness." Omnivorously attentive people are aware of the brisk air in their lungs, the firmness, wetness, warmness, and realness of their surroundings. More than that, omnivorously attentive people embrace the awe that such realness should induce.

We need omnivorously attentive people like Lewis in our lives to remind us of what we miss by sleep-walking. God is at work in a real, beautiful way every day, all day. Chesterton was a brother to Lewis in this regard. He put it this way: "Do not let the eye rest. Why should the eye be so lazy? Let us exercise the eye until it learns to see the startling facts that run across the landscape as clear as a painted face. Let us be ocular athletes" (*Tremendous Trifles*).

And I remember that Vietnamese boy somersaulting into the river—attentive, acrobatic, dexterous. We too can become ocular athletes, omnivorously attentive.

THE EYES OF SIMEON

Josef Pieper suggested that we have lost the skill to see because there is too much to absorb in the world. The eye is so inundated that it can no longer distinguish what should, and should not, claim our attention. It takes a special dedication and a measure of time away from visual stimulation for the imagination to start seeing again, seeing the way God sees.

If we practice this spiritual sightedness all of our days, then we will have the eyes of Simeon, who saw God in a baby overlooked by everyone else. We find his remarkable encounter with Mary and Joseph in the second chapter of Luke. When it was time for the purification practices required by the Law of Moses, they took Jesus to Jerusalem. To everyone else, Mary and Joseph were just another mom and dad taking their child to the temple. But not to Simeon. He had faithfully been looking, learning to see as God sees. He saw behind the appearance of things. And when the time came, God gave him prophetic words to declare.

Simeon is given to us as an example. He aligned his imagination to God's vision and work. That seems to me to be a harder and harder task the older we get. How easy to drift, to let inattention win the day. We need not live that way. Like Simeon, we can learn to see as God sees, to embrace all of the ordinariness of life, to see the hands and feet and face of God when others do not.

BENEDICTION

Through the mysterious work of the Holy Spirit, may he give you eyes of faith—a sacramental imagination. May your life's work help others to look, touch, taste, and digest the Christ. May it peel the scales from our eyes, lead us to new mountain heights, and reveal the extraordinary ordinary. May God lead you in the way everlasting (Ps. 139:24).

GRATUITOUS BEAUTY

"The world is charged with the grandeur of God.
It will flame out, like shining from shook foil . . ."
—Gerard Manley Hopkins, "God's Grandeur"

A sliver of moon rises above the dogwood tree, your siblings are tucked in bed, and a quiet has settled over the house. Your mom is busily at work in the other room and so I'm using the time, again, to jot down some thoughts that sprang to mind during the day.

When you were about three years old, we took you camping on the Olympic Peninsula. We rented a car for the first time and enjoyed riding in luxury all the way. Upon arrival, your mother and I gave you clear ground rules for the campground. No wandering off. No getting too near the fire. And no throwing rocks at the rental car. So far as I can recall, you did pretty well.

But on the morning of our return home, I glanced up from rolling the tent to see you scratching the car with a rock: intricate circles that swirled into expansive loops. I may have actually levitated on my way to save the car, but you were surprised at my urgency when I snatched the stone from your little hands. You said, "Daddy, I was painting a pretty picture."

Even before you could write words, you saw every surface—book pages, walls, desk surfaces, even shiny rental cars—as an opportunity to create something beautiful. Do you remember sneaking my books off of the shelf to underline and scribble notes in the margins? I do. I still open some of my beloved books to find your scrawled pen marks covering the pages.

As you know, you come from a long line of women on both sides of the family who care about beauty, goodness, and truth—even in little things. One of my first memorable encounters with man-made beauty was when I noticed my mother's cursive handwriting. Her smooth, looping strokes fascinated me. Their beauty called to something deep inside my six-year-old heart. What a strange thing to remember after all of these years, but it has stuck with me. My mother may not have known it at the time, but she was offering beauty to anyone who happened to read her letters, including her son. Her cursive, not just the letter's content, beckoned her reader. That is how beauty works. It calls to us, drawing the heart.

BEAUTY'S MYSTERIOUS POWER

Beauty affects everyone in this mysterious, immeasurable way. We burst into tears, or suddenly stand silent, or swell with childish happiness at its advent, but we can't seem to explain why. Even a brief exposure to its slightest expression vibrates the heart's strings.

Beauty also seems to play an important role in the insatiable human pursuit of fulfillment. Like metal shavings converging on a magnet, we gravitate toward beauty regardless of our differences—racial, economic, or otherwise. Truth may inform us, goodness may guide us, but beauty elicits a primordial longing in us. Beauty feels like home.

HUMANITY'S RESTLESS PURSUIT OF BEAUTY

According to Thomas Aquinas, the beautiful is whole, harmonious, and radiant (*Summa Theologiae I.xxxix.8*). It embodies everything our souls lack. Without it, we feel incomplete, restless, adrift. We feel uneasy, a spiritual and relational dissonance. Life often feels meaningless, earthbound, and dull. We long for wholeness, for harmony, and for radiance. Is it any wonder that we throw ourselves into the pursuit of beauty?

When our relationship with God was severed in the garden of Eden, our relationship with beauty was also severed. We lost the ability to see it clearly, to distinguish between kinds of beauty, to hold beauty and keep it. Now we only catch glimpses of it.

Beauty, like a ghostly vision, wanders city streets and blooming hills. Like a pixie, it plays hard to catch. Sometimes it takes an unexpected form. At other times, it hides entirely.

In our desperate hunger for beauty, we give our hearts away for fool's gold—something pretty and shiny, something svelte and smooth. Sooner or later we discover that our fool's gold is not the real thing. But the search continues. We find shapeshifters who take beauty's likeness but they do not satisfy and, again, we taste disappointment. Beauty relentlessly calls the human heart, so restlessness defines us.

I have wandered far and wide, from city streets to distant wilderness. Sometimes I glimpse beauty, sometimes I see only a likeness. I've been deceived by a thousand different shapeshifters in my life. My heart's unquenchable thirst for beauty indicates that my soul is still searching for its source, plunging after anything that faintly reminds me of my spiritual home, restless until I find my rest in God (Augustine, *Confessions*).

God is the soul's magnetic pole. We remain unfulfilled until we find him. But even those who have found God know that any given moment finds us closer or farther away from him. We're never unbrokenly united with him, not in this life.

PRIMARY AND SECONDARY BEAUTY

So wherever it wanders, the soul's trajectory is either closer to God's beauty or farther away. God is primary Beauty. Every other expression of beauty is secondary, like smaller, more manageable bites of an ultimate whole. His creation—all this roiling life—testifies to The Artist and to his beauty, leaving road signs pointing toward him. None of them are the destination.

None of them can satisfy because none of them are the object of our longing. They all say, "Not here, not yet."

That's one reason why the world is simultaneously full of such deep, entrancing pleasures and such startling disappointments. We have not reached our destination, we have only experienced a foretaste. Food, entertainment, technological gadgets, sex, friendship, vacation—none of them last. No matter how tightly we grip, satisfaction evades us. Why? Because these experiences are only signs, footprints left in the sand by Beauty himself.

Persistently dedicated to satisfaction, people chase pleasure until it is no longer pleasurable. If we glut ourselves on these secondary expressions of beauty, we find ourselves bloated and sick. Joy will forever evade us as long as personal pleasure is the only source of our happiness. Our imaginations will slumber in a deluge of sensual overload as they pursue a life-time of drunken obsession with pleasure. We need the sanctified imagination— the eye of the soul—to see where all these signposts are pointing. And we need faith to follow the path.

God likes to use writers to open eyes and align imaginations to himself. The best writers give us glimpses of primary beauty, visions of splendor. Generative writers are called to this glorious work, so they value beauty and lean into it, finding every way possible to orient their imaginations to God's primary beauty. They read God's word, sing his songs, play with children, and learn from scientists. They read theology and poetry, remembering all along that the goal is not beauty, but God himself.

Some people turn beauty into a means for self-fulfillment and others claim to love beauty for its own sake, but Christian writers love beauty for God's sake. They prioritize the pursuit of God over the mere pursuit of beauty, but they recognize beauty's important role in that divine pursuit. They also recognize that *pretty* can be microwaved, but beauty takes time. Instead of driving fast cars or flinging their hearts at every hot date, generative writers crouch to see beauty up close. They stoop to catch it, like a child sneaking up on a dragonfly.

While beauty touches all of us, generative writers try to hold it, channel it, replicate it, transform it in their own lives and in the lives of those they meet. Your deep impulse and sacred calling is to treat your life and work with an artist's deep respect, carefully learning to see the artistic handiwork of God and participate in it.

According to Revelation 1:6, God's children are kings and priests in the world, but Christian writers live out this calling in unique ways. In some ways, writers stand in front of the people to lead in a particular direction like a king, or, like a priest, to lead in worship and praise. Their work is a prayer offered to God. Like kings and priests, their labor takes a toll on them. They sacrifice their time, their energy, even their emotional and mental well-being for the sake of God's people. The entirety of a generative writer's life points toward this kind of sacrificially beautiful and beautifying work. It is the writer's vocational expectation and priestly duty to track the evidence of God's gratuitous beauty in the world, to embody it, and to nourish it in others.

INHABITING BEAUTY

As a little girl, you spent hours building fairy gardens in the back yard. Houses with their own small gardens, barns with tiny hay bales. You carved out streams and planted miniature woodlands across from miniature fields. You were building for the sheer pleasure of building, doing what people of all ages do—transforming your world into something habitable.

The word "habit" once meant clothing, one's attire. To inhabit meant to climb inside those clothes and live there. If something is habitable, it is wearable. To inhabit a home means more than simply to reside there. One may reside at a hotel room, but one inhabits a home. Artists of every stripe are trying to make their world more habitable. I would encourage you to do more than just make your world more habitable, make it more habitable for all of us.

Your effectiveness in that effort will depend upon your intimacy with beauty. It will depend on whether you have allowed beauty to mold you. Have you spent so much time with beauty that beauty's nuances and mysteries now form and inform you according to its unbridled and nonlinear nature? Its effect upon you will be gradual. Waking one day, you will realize that its effect upon your intuitions, orientations, and sightedness has occurred mysteriously. A boy who lives his entire life in the wind-blown prairies of Montana does not realize their influence upon him until he tries to live in the closed spaces of New York City. Our physical and geographical spaces subtly shape the way we think, feel, and move.

Beauty works upon us in a similar fashion. Be content with the reality that we cannot grasp beauty like a child holds a flower. We can't even grasp beauty like we can grasp a logical argument. But we can inhabit it. We can wrap it around us. The mind absorbs beauty more than it understands it and that absorption works upon the heart like your home life works upon yours. Be patient with beauty's persistent but gradual influence. And be intentional about seeking its influence upon your life.

GATHERING AND GENERATING BEAUTY

Perhaps the medieval view of creativity can inform your pursuit of generativity. The honeybee gathers pollen widely, then it processes the pollen and creates something entirely different that is sweet to the tongue: honey. Medieval thinkers recognized the honeybee's activity as an apt picture of the mind's activity: the healthy mind gathers information, processes it, and then creates something new and different. Writers live this way all the time. They read and converse widely, internalizing and transforming information and conversations into the honey of a new work which is pleasurable and a gift to others.

The medieval bee metaphor explains why generative writers do not rest like some people. Their hearts and minds work continuously even while reclining on a summer day. Some people can shut down their brains and suntan on the dock, but writers find it difficult, if not impossible, to do so. Writers perpetually wrestle with how to beautify their work, how to better image forth God's ineffable beauty.

BEAUTY IN A UTILITARIAN WORLD

The work required to hold, channel, replicate, and transform beauty is challenging. It requires more time, attention, patience, and skill than most people are willing to give. Staying awake to and observant of God's gratuitous giftings strains even the best of us. Perhaps the difficulty of staying awake is proof of its immense importance.

Unfortunately, you're growing up in a world awash in utilitarianism. Many people are so busy that they only care about useful creations. They want the latest gadget or app that saves them time. But beauty does not save time, it gives time meaning. And your writing gives meaning to others in a mysterious, unquantifiable and impractical way.

If a thing's value hinges only upon its usefulness, then beauty has no place in our lives. The consequences of this view are many, including the exile of artists who traffic in beauty. A people who trade beauty for practicality have forgotten the preeminent artist, God. In fact, they may inadvertently usher him right out of their daily lives—leaving themselves abandoned to sterile confines and heartless gadgets.

When did we forget that God is an artist? How have we forgotten that he made a world he did not need, most of which we do not need either. It's true that our world contains billions of fragile macro- and micro-ecosystems which depend one upon the other, but I still say that the sheer number of swallows careening through the air outside my window at this moment is proof that God pays little mind to utility. He takes pleasure in lavishing the world with beauty and charging our existence with his glory and grace and generosity, with his gratuitous beauty.

PRAISE HIM

The more that beauty forms and informs us, the more cause we will have to praise God. The penultimate purpose of the Christian life is uncomplicated: give glory to God and enjoy him throughout life. Christian writers have the same purpose. The human heart naturally rolls downhill toward worry, complaint, and frustration. Praise and true enjoyment of God require intention. They do not come to us easily; we must push them up the mountain as we climb. Only after many years of doing so will we find that they are pulling us up—and that just in time. By then we will be nearing the climb's steepest grade where praise and enjoyment are most necessary.

This poem by Rainer Maria Rilke speaks directly to poets, but also to all writers whose work is deliberate:

> O tell us, poet, what you do. —I praise.
> Yes, but the deadly and the monstrous phase,
> how do you take it, how resist? —I praise.
> But the anonymous, the nameless maze,

how summon it, how call it, poet? —I praise.
What right is yours, in all these varied ways,
under a thousand masks yet true? —I praise.
And why do stillness and the roaring blaze,
both star and storm acknowledge you? —because I praise.

No matter the hardship, no matter the bewilderment, Christian writers learn to see the relentless torrent of God's blessing and panoply of beauty —to stand beneath it, relish its refreshment, and raise their hearts in praise.

BENEDICTION

Wherever God leads you, whatever your circumstances, may you remain unspoiled by the world's tinsel toys. May you forever stand beneath God's gratuitous beauty and give thanks for so many cascading gifts—the magnificent and the miniscule. May you learn beauty's subtleties—the wondrous and the beloved, the textured and the luminous, the transcendent and the ordinary. May you watch for the delicate and the overlooked. A word. A glance. A gesture of grace.

THE CRAFTSMAN'S WAY

"The world's best work, in the schools as in the shops, is done by the calm, steady, persistent efforts of skilled workmen who know how to keep their tools sharp, and to make every effort reach its mark."
—John Milton Gregory, *The Seven Laws of Teaching*

When I was a boy, reluctantly learning the writing craft, I loved using adjectives. They filled the page nicely. I liked the cleverness and ease of writing a sentence like, "The tall, dark-haired old man drove his old, yellow, rusty Chevrolet car to the old, red grocery store." I did not agree with the likes of Mark Twain who said, "When you catch an adjective, kill it." My mother tried to stifle my infatuation with adjectives. The chorus of teachers that followed tried, too. And now my editors do the same. I'm a slow learner. While I still struggle with an over-reliance on adjectives, I know that they can often water down the noun, especially when it comes to the adjective "Christian."

I've been forced in conversation to use "Christian" in association with the words "artist" and "writer" because I'm both a Christian and a writer. But I'm conflicted every time. Something feels out of whack when I describe myself as a "Christian writer." I think this is why:

No one, not even a Christian, asks for a "Christian" surgeon to help when the heart fails; a good surgeon is all we desire. Or, upon encountering a beautiful garden, we make no assumptions about the gardener's religion; we simply acknowledge the master gardener's skill. The same can be said of plumbers, metal fabricators, cobblers, and car designers. Each of these vocations demands a certain amount of creativity, like an artist, but for these fields we simply demand an honest and skilled fabricator. The same should be asked of writers.

A CHRISTIAN WRITER'S DISTINGUISHING CONVICTIONS

Writers should write well. The adjective "Christian" applies not so much to the work we do (unless its focus is expressly religious), but to our allegiance and to our convictions. Every writer holds convictions, a Christian writer simply holds Christian ones. I hold firmly to the Apostle's Creed. I aim to glorify God (Ps. 86:12), to enjoy him forever. I aim to love God with all my heart, soul, mind, and strength. And I aim to love my neighbor as I love myself. These are not unique to me, they describe all orthodox Christians.

But to list some of the key descriptions of a Christian writer would look something like this:

1. Christian writers testify to the mystery and glory, transcendence and immanence, of God. Their lives and work—whether poem, story, or journal article—harmonize with these themes.

2. Christian writers practice thinking God's thoughts after him. Though their work may spring from the muck of suffering or the rot of regret, yet it mysteriously sings a song of praise that reveals the hidden depth of souls well-anchored in the rock of God's promises.

3. Christian writers believe that they are sent. Like the Apostle in Acts 26:16-18, they minister to believers and unbelievers alike. They serve and heal, bearing witness to the things which they have seen and the things which are yet to be revealed.

4. Christian writers have the Holy Spirit in their eyes, in their mouths, and in their pens. What they see, what they say, and what they write correspond with the testimony given in God's word.

5. Christian writers have the Christian story coursing through their blood, a story centered on death and resurrection. A story framed by creation, fall, and redemption.

What do you notice about this list? It's not really distinctive to writers, is it? It could describe anyone loyal to Christ, regardless of vocation. And none of these important convictions alter the fundamental demand for quality work.

VOCATION: TO CALL

We get the word "vocation" from the Latin word *vocare* which means "to call." Christians recognize that their calling is the work of continuing what Christ began, and we do so in every sphere of life. Every job is a ministry. Some people see their work as no more than a job that pays the bills, but because Christians serve Jesus, their work should be a divine call—no matter the vocation. In Christ, being a chef or an accountant or a factory worker is being an emissary of God. Whether well-paid or not, their service acts as an extension of Christ's heart and hands.

This is the wide-lens perspective: we get to continue Christ's cultural work in every station of life. But when it comes to deciding where we can do that work best, many of us quaver under the pressure to make the right decision. We pray and agonize over which college to choose or where to pursue a day job. Yet the wide-lens perspective gives us freedom at this level, too. God's law provides a boundary line within which we're free to eagerly and happily do what we love to do.

So whether writing or doing any other job, whether marrying someone or moving across the country, go through the steps that any decision requires and then step out in faith. Pray for wisdom. Seek wisdom. Submit your impulses to wisdom's voice. Listen carefully to the advice of those who know you best and those who have walked the path you are considering. If it has to do with a career move, for example, you have some simple questions to answer: Does the job fall within God's law? Is it fitting to your abilities and personality? Are there obligations you would be neglecting? What do those who know you best suggest you do? Would you love doing it? Are you at an age when many people are tempted to make bad decisions? Weigh these things. Big decisions require time. Your grandfather had a Two-Week Rule he forced upon me at an early age: if I wanted something (a watch, a pair of shoes, a bike), I had to wait two weeks before buying it or asking for it. He knew my desire for the object would probably wane and if I bought it rashly, I would likely not value it. If the longing lasted two weeks, then it might be worth pursuing. The Two-Week Rule only really applies to smaller decisions, but the principle applies to all choices you make in life. Praying for wisdom, pursuing wisdom, and submitting your impulses to wisdom requires time. Be patient.

THE CALL TO SET OUT FOR AN UNKNOWN PLACE

When it comes to writing, heed what John Calvin called "the inner and outer call." If you feel compelled to write and if those who read your work encourage you to keep writing, then you should write. The same goes for *what* you write. If you feel compelled to write a particular story and those you respect encourage you to do so, then write the story. If a poem, write the poem. If an op-ed article, write the article.

But the call for artists is not always straightforward. In fact, it often sounds more like God's call to Abraham to set out for an unknown place (Eugene Peterson, *For the Beauty of the Church*) not knowing where you're going (Heb. 11:8), or Paul's call from Christ to get up and enter the city and wait to be told what to do (Acts 9:6). It is the call that Christ gave to his friends to deny themselves, take up their crosses, and follow him (Matt. 16:24). Who is prepared for this calling? Who has the courage without God's emboldening Spirit? None of us.

Yes, we often feel ill-equipped, a bit bewildered, and unqualified to continue Christ's work as writers. We would rather give that title to so-and-so. They would do a much better job anyway, or so we think. But God has called us to this generational, inspirational, and generous work. So we can trust that he will equip us for the task if we keep focusing on quality work.

Your job is to hone your skills as a writer. Remember that excellent work reflects an excellent God. Gain a reputation for exceptional work, be precise and thorough, become reliable for quality and insightfulness. Whatever your genre, learn from the best. Ask lots of questions. Practice. Fail. Then try again. Perfect your skills. Learning is part of a craftsman's job description, and questions are the whole of learning. In my twenty years of teaching, I've found this maxim true: good students ask good questions. A good craftsman is a good student of the craft.

THE MARKS OF A CRAFTSMAN

The Palpant family line includes several generations of wood-carvers. They are artisans whose blade-and-chisel art is a uniquely geometric and intricate woodwork called chip carving. Their wooden trays, grandfather clocks, and side tables mesmerized me when I was young and do so still. Such artistry requires great patience and remarkable attention to detail.

Those two traits—patience and attention—seem to me the most important attributes of a craftsman. And they distinguish the craftsman's lasting work from the disposable work that crowds our marketplaces. How many of us have that kind of patience or that attention span anymore? How many realize that the quality of our work reflects upon the God we worship. If you would be a generative writer, you will need to think like a craftsman.

MODERNITY AND CRAFTSMANSHIP

Unfortunately, the modern pace of life and the myriad distractions at our fingertips discourage the character traits necessary for craftsmanship. Many people fritter away their time rather than spend it intentionally. Others live in perpetual survival mode and have no margin for careful creation. Few will be able to look back and say, "I made that." Craftsmen will.

That sense of accomplishment has a remarkable effect upon a person's heart and mind. It casts a happy mantle over the past, giving meaning to a person's life. And it is meaning that propels a person to further action in the world. You will need that sense of accomplishment for spiritual, emotional, and mental well-being as a writer. But you cannot have it by just writing anything, you need to have written something well. That is the craftsman's way.

Craftsmen do not fear hard work. They do not shun the discipline required for meaningful accomplishment. Instead, they concentrate on precision and grace, not scattering their energies, but aiming them toward the completion of the consecrated task. They know that great work is done by steady, determined, focused people who keep their tools sharp and their efforts well-aimed. Craftsmen know that patience is a hallmark of quality. They attend to details, arranging and executing them with careful attention. They exemplify the secret joy found in work well done.

Even the Preacher in Ecclesiastes started with good craftsmanship in writing his sermons: "And moreover, because the Preacher was wise, he still taught the people knowledge; yes, he pondered and sought out and set in order many proverbs. The Preacher sought to find acceptable words; and what was written was upright—words of truth. The words of the wise are like goads, and the words of scholars are like well-driven nails, given by one Shepherd" (Ecc. 12:9-11). Christian writers imitate that preacher in their careful arrangement of words and their habits.

HABITS ARE THE HALLMARK OF SUCCESS

Successful writers know that habits are the hallmark of their success. What appears to others as giftedness is instead the result of devoted thinking and regular work, patient attention to a skill over a long period of time. A craftsman's instincts are informed by years of practiced and principled thought and work, habits of mind and hand. Inspiration only gets us off of the runway; habits keep us airborne. Legacies are formed on the back of good habits in the mundane. They belong to those who sustain effort, to those who focus. Over time, you will see that success has more to do with good habits and less to do with raw talent. You will also notice that most failures can be traced back to poor habits. The difference between mediocrity and greatness is consistency.

How many parents think of those ramifications while raising their sons and daughters? When their son complains about discipline or restrictions or an unwanted workload, parents would do well to say, "I'm serving your future self." Alexander Pope once said that "just as the twig is bent the tree's inclined." His words suggest that we're too casual about the habits we develop while young. Habits are always hard to break—both the bad ones and the good ones—and they impact us in lasting and immeasurable ways. Attend to yours. The following list of generative habits for quality work is neither exhaustive nor in any particular order, but I hope they are helpful.

HABIT I: WAKE EARLY

As the motto goes, "Win the morning, win the day." God has given you much more discretionary time than you think. This freedom demands discipline and character. Given the freedom to drowse or to work, most people would drowse. Talent, desire, strength, and vision rapidly erode in those who drowse. Use your time well.

HABIT 2: WORK EVERY DAY

Maya Angelou famously said, "Nothing will work unless you do." If able, try to work a little every day, including Saturday. Take Sundays off, of course, as a celebration of rest, but spread your work out over the other six. Some lines of work make this impossible, but steady work is better for a person than working in fits and starts. Be methodical. Does that sound boring? Fine. Boring, steady, habitual work is the path to excellence. A steady, unflattering pace is necessary for a craftsman who wants her work to outlast her own lifetime.

HABIT 3: PRAY

Jim Elliot rightly said, "That saint who advances on his knees never retreats." A generative life depends upon steady mental, emotional, and spiritual advancement. For the Christian, generativity is impossible apart from God's grace to sustain, guide, and inspire— hence our need to pray. Prayer time is tank-filling time. Writing will demand your best wisdom, and your deepest courage. It will require discernment and vulnerability. It will tax your determination, your emotional and mental capacities, and, depending on the nature of your work, your very soul. You will feel naked, exposed to inclement weather: wind, fog, and sleet. What you write articulates your very person, it is the shining forth of your soul. The quality of your soul rests on the quality of your prayer life.

HABIT 4: TAKE WALKS

Enter the day with the sun's rising or escort the evening long enough to feel some of the clamor, struggle, and status fall away. Walking allows time for uninterrupted prayer and the steadying of one's chaotic thoughts. Walking allows room for decompression. For the generative person, it is also a time when ideas long silent in one's heart, like a seed, sometimes germinate.

HABIT 5: COURT YOUR CALLING

Marriages that survive are built on time together and attention to one another. Spouses who court each other sincerely and purposefully, enjoy long and lasting marriages. The same principle goes for piano, business, sports, and writing. Courtship demands time, not just convenient time. Spend lots of time honing your skills and you will see results. In the same way you would court your beloved, court your craft. Love it patiently and it will love you in return.

HABIT 6: PAY ATTENTION

One barrier to completing any project is distraction. Close the door both literally and metaphorically; close the door on the phone, social media, and errands that suddenly multiply in your head. From beginning to end, stay locked in on the work. Don't let unnecessary distraction hijack the quality and pace of the task at hand.

HABIT 7: STAY GROUNDED

Some people aim for excellent craftsmanship so they can win fame. They are vainglorious even before they have earned any significant praise. Quality craftsmanship requires a humble focus on the task at hand without aiming for fan letters. Craftsmanship prioritizes faithfulness. It esteems small but regular acts of creation that most people overlook as mundane. Those small deeds really add up over time. God built the world in such a way that small and overlooked acts hold immeasurable potential. Behold the acorn. Behold the human cell. Mighty works like *Moby Dick* begin small, with one letter. And heavenly music like Chopin's "Prelude in E Minor" begins with one note. Forget about fame, focus on the work.

HABIT 8: PLAY

Your mind is like any muscle and functions best under just the right tension. Over-working the muscle causes breakdown.

Therefore, engage in other activities without worrying that you're robbing yourself of work time. Learning to pace ourselves is a lifelong study. Paint. Vacuum. Bake bread. Take walks. Study a language. Read for pleasure. Sit on the porch and talk with your grandparents. Color with your little sister. You will find that kind of alternate exertion helpful to the craftsman life.

HABIT 9: CULTIVATE YOUR REASON

The life of the mind is immensely important in Christianity. God's call to love him with all of your mind is as important as the call to love him with your heart and soul and strength. We reason well or reason poorly, but we always reason. Learn to think logically and be sure to align your logic with God's. Think accurately and precisely. Know how to follow a logical thought all the way to its conclusion. Practice uncommon perspicuity. Careful thinking leads to careful work.

HABIT 10: FINISH THE WORK

Starting and finishing are difficult. You can fail by never starting and you can fail by not finishing. Most of us fail because we never close the deal. We run out of steam or get distracted. Finish something and you've already accomplished more than most people. And having done so, you will feel a satisfaction necessary for continued production, so finish.

Michelangelo's teacher apparently told his students that talent is cheap, but dedication is costly. He knew that the hardest parts of the highest work are discipline and determination, not inspiration. Excellent work requires attention to detail and an unrelenting pursuit of one's best.

My grandfather had a verse framed in his bedroom and I grew up with it inextricably associated with his work ethic: "Do you see a man who excels in his work? He will stand before kings; he will not stand before unknown men" (Prov. 22:29). He rightly believed that a skilled artist—a craftsman—is honored in due time.

Although it may feel as though you have been on this mountain trek for a long time, you have only just begun. Don't be discouraged. Here at the outset of your ascent, look to the Author and Finisher of your faith, the dream weaver. Keep silent before him, still and awake. He will take you by the hand and keep you. He will give you what you need when you need it.

BENEDICTION

May God give you sustained patience and attention to detail. May he teach you the ways of a craftsman, guiding your mind and hands into quality work. May your life be characterized by quiet confidence, not harried energy. Most of all, may your life habits lead you into the kind of work that even you could not imagine possible.

LEARNING TO REST

"It is vain for you to rise up early, to sit up late, to eat the bread of sorrows; for so he gives his beloved sleep."
—Psalm 127:2

I used to sleep in my truck during lunch breaks. Not every day, but especially during basketball season, I did it quite often. Teaching full time, coaching a varsity basketball team, raising three children, leading the deacons at my church, and writing in my spare time took their toll. I rightly understood the high value God placed on people in his kingdom and had prioritized service in everything I did, but failed to calculate for sleep. I had no theology of rest.

By all appearances, my life goal was to burn hot and burn out to the glory of God. Longevity had taken a back seat to urgency. When my father gently suggested I reconsider my sleep habits, I did not. The doctors who have walked with me through my subsequent health struggles point to poor sleep as a major contributor. True, some of my sleep issues are outside of my direct control, but I've not paid proper attention to rest. Generative faithfulness and generative longevity depend upon learning to rest physically, emotionally, and mentally. A theology of rest is not optional for you; it is necessary.

IMITATE GOD IN YOUR RESTING AND WORKING

Just as God worked, we should work. Just as God rested, we should rest. God never calls work an inconvenience. And he never calls rest the ultimate good. His work in Genesis 1 is generative work, but his rest on the seventh day is also generative rest. It did not signal the end of his labors, nor was it the final aim of all his work. He is our example. We, too, should work hard enough that rest is necessary, and we should rest to prepare for further work.

Some people don't know how to rest. Others idealize it. We run the risk of forgetting that God made us to work effectively. Those who don't rest may sacrifice their health, their family, and their longevity for short term gain. On the other hand, those who don't work—those who long for vacation—may sacrifice a meaningful, generative life in favor of comfort.

Either way, this flip of priorities runs counter to the generative life. Our priority is long term, faithful work that glorifies God and serves people generationally, inspirationally, and generously. Work is not inimical to rest, but the wrong kind of rest is inimical to work. Despite the advertisements that indoctrinate otherwise, rest is actually rejuvenation time for further work, not merely a reward for work finished. The steady advance of a writer's life depends upon this proper view of work and rest.

AIMING HIGH ENOUGH

So what are the obstacles to resting rightly? One possible problem is that we don't have high aspirations. Our goals, if we have any, are easily achievable. A low aim inspires lethargy. An achievable but difficult aim inspires work. A lofty goal gives us purpose and meaning. It is the stimulant that awakens our hopes and inspires our best efforts. By reaching for it, we sometimes achieve more than we would have otherwise. It is the difficulty of an endeavor that often compels us to achievement and brings with it emotional, mental, and spiritual vitality. No one ever felt fulfilled chasing a participation certificate, so your vitality as a writer will rise to the difficulty of your project. You will find that the difficulty itself refreshes your vigor far better than shuffling around the house aimlessly seeking another amusement. The scriptures say that work is good and that work finished well brings its own reward (Prov. 14:23). Worthwhile work is, indeed, a blessing from God. It inflames the heart.

RECOGNIZING WHAT IS OUT OF OUR CONTROL

Another reason we don't rest effectively is that we want controllable, measurable, and immediate results for our work. Those are achievable when you build fast food burgers, but impossible when writing. We work ourselves into the ground trying to force or predict results. Or we fritter away our energies on diagnostics and social trends, trying to anticipate how our writing will be received instead of getting down to work. Do not work too hard at predicting business trends, or societal and cultural changes. The world's changeability need not dictate your labor. Work. Leave the prosperity to God.

RESTING THE HEART, NOT JUST THE MIND AND BODY

It is never enough to simply rest the body and the mind. The heart needs rest, too. Our emotions shape the nature of our fatigue—whether physical, mental, or spiritual. The body, mind, and heart work together, inextricably. Recuperation, therefore, must involve the whole person. Any number of things can cause fatigue and sometimes the true cause is not directly visible.

We have grown up in a society that generally holds to one form of rest: dissipation. We trudge through the week and then squander our energies on the weekend. But people are like first-rate cellos. They require loosening and tightening, not unstringing, if they are to sing as they were designed. They need to stay well-tuned if they are to function best. Cellos demand steady, deliberate care. You need the same.

A frenetic pace and a frantic mindset rob the heart's soil of its nutrients and leave nothing but exhaustion. Life chaos is usually symptomatic of soul chaos. Not always, but often. The

Psalmist reminds us that a restless, relentless life is barren: "It is vain for you to rise up early, to sit up late, to eat the bread of sorrows; for so he gives his beloved sleep" (Ps. 127:2).

Writing can feel remarkably unrewarding, unpredictable, and exhausting. How much more important, then, to go about the work as deliberately and as paced as possible? To weave sabbath rests into each day? The generative life is impossible if we're perpetually fatigued.

CALIBRATING TO THE DEMANDS OF THE GENERATIVE LIFE

Novice writers are often surprised by the physical and mental taxation of writing for long lengths of time. They need time to acclimate to the disciplined rigors of focused writing. The work is draining, no doubt. We lose confidence. But the heart and mind calibrate to the demands over time. Persevere, patiently recognizing the need for more experience.

In time, you will adapt to the rhythms, work hours, and demands of writing. Effective work is always accomplished by the steady application of pressure on mind, heart, and hands. When all three work in step with each other, writing grows vibrant and resilient. All three must be focused. If your mind wanders off, your writing will be shoddy. If your heart disengages, your writing will feel lethargic. If your hands get lazy, your writing will never get done.

The writing life requires this forward lean. We do our best work when we feel positive, hopeful, determined, and patient.

When we don't rest well, we feel discouraged, demotivated, and impatient. Rest well. Does the writing life tire you now? Do not fret. You will adapt. Learn to persist and remember that persistence is impossible without adequate rest. Keep writing, but learn how to rest.

BENEDICTION

Sertillanges once wrote, "I sleep; Nature keeps watch; God keeps watch, and tomorrow I shall gather a little of the fruit of their work. In this quiet spirit, you relax completely, more than if you thought anxiously of a morrow without help, more above all than by living over again at night, as so often happens, the worries of the day." May God give you the strength to rest and to endure. May he give you a measured pace. May he give you margin for rest and may he teach you how to do so. God says, "In returning and rest you shall be saved; in quietness and confidence shall be your strength" (Isa. 30:15). May you rest well to work well.

LISTEN

"I think that art has something to do with an arrest of attention in the midst of distraction."

—Saul Bellow

On a recent road trip, I heard a distant thumping sound like a helicopter. It came and went for awhile, but the frequency increased. Soon the sound was not only more frequent, but loud enough that I thought the helicopter was following us.

"What are you looking for," my wife asked.

"I'm looking for that helicopter," I said.

"What helicopter?" she asked.

"Can't you hear that whirring, thumping sound?" I asked.

"Nope."

We both turned to you in the back seat and asked you to moderate our argument: "You hear it, right?" I asked. You sided with your mother.

I was dumbfounded. How could you not hear it? We had driven several hours when the sound got loud enough for me to locate it in the front of the car. I pulled the car over, but found nothing wrong. Still, neither of you could hear the sound. I noticed that the sound increased at certain speeds and decreased when I maintained a slower speed. But soon enough, the thumping got so loud that I thought something would fall apart. Only then did you and your mother finally hear it.

When we arrived at our destination, I described the sound to a mechanic. "Does it sound like a distant helicopter?" he asked.

"Yes! Exactly like that," I said.

"Well," he said casually, "your rotor needs replaced." He was right.

We have since discovered that my health issues include something called hyperacusis, an increased sensitivity to the volume and frequencies of sound. It is an undesirable affliction, unless you need to hear something that most people miss. It seems to me that this story has a spiritual parallel. Christians—especially Christian writers—are called to listen even more carefully to higher spiritual frequencies, to hear what most people somehow miss.

LISTENING IN THE DARK

When Jesus sent his disciples to their work in the world, he told them, "Whatever I tell you in the dark, speak in the light; and what you hear in the ear, preach on the housetops" (Matt. 10:27). This is a layered verse worthy of much contemplation. What is your dark corner? There, in the darkness, listen. What comprises your darkness? Is it literal darkness? Listen. Do you find yourself awake in the middle of the night and wonder why? Maybe that is an invitation to listen. Perhaps your darkness, like mine, is largely metaphorical. Come, let us listen in our loneliness, our shame, our bewilderment. God is never silent. Even there in the closet where we cry, let us listen.

I'm inclined to think that if God spoke to Balaam by way of a donkey, to David by way of a drunk, and to John in a voice that sounded like thunder, then he can speak to us as he so chooses and where he so chooses—even in the dark. But preparing ourselves to hear him requires cultivating that habit.

LISTENING IN A NOISY WORLD

On this climb up the mountain of faith, I've slowly realized that my practices do not often match my aims. For example, I often want sincerity, discernment, and insightfulness without the lifestyle that develops them. My appetites have adjusted to the society in which I live and are accustomed now to speed and noise. "I don't have time to read God's word, to take a walk, or to sit still," I tell myself.

Even now, as I sit beside my mountain path to rest, I forget to imitate Elijah who once sat on a mountain, too. Bundled in a ragged quilt, he shivered in his mountain cave one night.

Gale force winds howled outside the cave's entrance, but the Lord was not in the wind. Soon followed an earthquake, but the Lord was not in that either. Even when a forest fire raged up the mountain, the Lord was not in it. But in the charred, smoky silence that followed, the Lord spoke quietly, and when Elijah heard that voice he came to the entrance and stood still to listen (1 Kings 19:11-13). I long to listen in this way. I long to stand in my heart's cave, to wrap myself in humility, and to hear the voice of God.

REVERENCE AND HUMILITY

But just as I sense myself learning to hear, something swings me back into the whirl and push of self-absorbed activity. Is it my lack of reverence? If reverence is a deep regard for God and for everything that he created, surely I know my shortcomings! Dietrich von Hildebrand believed that all spiritual virtues spring from reverence, that it is the source of all clear perception and holy action. If the clarity of a life depends upon the clarity of one's perception, it would serve me well to practice this profound respect even in the most trivial hours of my days. Indeed, I will never hear what I don't care to hear.

For this very reason, humility precedes reverence. Humble people are teachable, willing to listen. They recognize their limitations, their need, their proper position at the feet of almighty God. Deep down, they care about their relationship with him and how they function within his created order.

Reverent writers testify to God's activity in life. The tone of their work runs counter to the run-of-the-mill self-gratification, praise-mongering, and sentimentality that generally floods the world. It also runs counter to those writers clamoring for attention—the caterwaulers, the braggadocious, even the "cultural critics" who specialize in rhetorical blunt-force trauma. Instead, people find reverent writers enchanting. Readers sense a higher form of sincerity, insightfulness, and discernment. These are the marks of generative writers.

SINCERITY AND INSIGHTFULNESS

Thomas Carlyle said, "It is a man's sincerity and depth of vision that makes him a Poet." And it's exactly these kinds of writers, those of sincerity and depth, that affirm life and enrich our experience of it. They offer a glimpse of the divine countenance, and because they listen well they testify to the invisible behind the visible universe.

So let me encourage you who likely feel neither reverent enough nor sincere enough. What you hear in secret, while submersed in silent intimacy with God, may seem insignificant and unprofound. It may seem utterly ordinary, but it will be valuable to those who read your work. So long as you're sharing those insights as a companion on life's journey, your insights will cement relationships in some way. Knowing that fact does not make writing any easier, but you will surely find that careful listening and honest expression of what you have heard in the dark gives your words weight even when those words feel flimsy to you.

Don't be in a hurry to give your words weight. You can't rush the process. Many young writers forget that insightfulness can't be faked very well. Wisdom comes by experience. Instead of having the patience to become a genuinely insightful person, a young writer may pretend to insights she has not tested through the passage of time. Instead of walking with the wise, listening to the wise, and reading the wise, many young writers focus on how many likes their latest social-network post received. They would rather be praised than become praiseworthy. They would rather sound deep than become deeper people. You will not be like them.

DISCERNMENT

Listening not only gives your soul depth, it also gives you ideas. An idea is a precious thing, however small. It is spark to the fire, seed to the tree, the indispensable beginning to all creative acts. A thousand ideas cross our minds each day, most of which we dismiss without a second thought. For writers, listening means discerning. Every generative artist knows that ideas somehow come from outside oneself, that we simply steward them and serve as the vehicle of their expression. But listening means saying yes to some ideas and saying no to others. Only by wisdom, prayer, and practice will you know what to listen for in the darkness and how to speak it for others to hear.

A writer's intuition is a precious commodity worth protecting and nurturing. Which idea do you follow? Which word do you use? And when? Which choice is necessary and which one is superfluous? The quality of your decisions reflects the quality of your intuition. The quality of your intuition reflects the quality of your listening. Be a listener.

LISTENING LIKE SAMUEL

Do you remember the Old Testament story of Samuel, of his time as a boy when he served in the temple? Can you see his small mattress on the stone floor? Can you see him lying on his back, hands clasped behind his head, awake in the dark? Even at a young age, his spirit was keenly tuned to God's voice. When he heard God call his name, Samuel responded. He experienced life with an ear for what God was saying in each moment, using those experiences faithfully for others. He became known for listening to God so carefully that it could be said of him, "He let none of [God's] words fall to the ground" (1 Sam. 3:19).

How I wish to imitate that child. May God speak to me in all the seasons of my life. May I seek his voice in the morning and in the evening, listening for him on dark days and on bright days. Hearing him in the storm and in the gentle breeze.

I would have you listen like that, too. Listen for God's voice like a woman who drops a stone down a dark abyss, her senses strained keenly to hear the moment it hits water. Like Samuel, you can be perceptive, acutely sensitive to the smallest spiritual vibration, awake to God's insights, not simply your own.

One of the more memorable plants of my childhood in Africa was the Angel's Trumpet. Its flower was large and white with a pungent aroma. The peculiar thing about this plant is that it blooms at night. Even on dark tropical nights, I could see the bright blooms outside my window. Under the right conditions, our hearts can bloom like that plant—in the darkness—poised upward, open-mouthed, eagerly awaiting God's inspiration.

Your devotional readings, your prayers, your daily conversations weave together while you sleep. And when you wake in the middle of the night, listen then, too. I have a friend who regularly finds himself suddenly awake at 3:00 AM. He told me he has slowly learned over the years that, "This is the time of God's voice in my life. He is speaking. I best be listening."

Let the scriptures echo in the caverns of your heart and mind. Listen to that echo. I would have you take the Holy Spirit's hand and inspect your inner landscapes. I would have you approach God's throne helplessly, yet expectantly. Someone once told me that A. W. Tozer would write on his knees, always in a posture of supplication. He wanted to think God's thoughts after him, to be a conduit for the water of life. You need not imitate him bodily, but your heart posture should be the same.

If, when we pray, we're told to enter our private spaces, close the door, and pray to our Father who is in secret, and if it is true that our Father sees us in that secret place and rewards those kinds of prayers, then we may consider what that reward might be. Perhaps the reward is simply a deeper intimacy with God, perhaps even an intuition, or maybe a word whose fragility and delicacy make it difficult to fully grasp. Listen carefully for the inclinations he gives to you.

EKSTASIS

Not every idea is the same. A very few contain the strength and heat to birth a new creation. Most of those begin with an epiphany, like a whisper in a dark room. This is the ultimate reward for learning to listen. Although some substantive ideas do not visit us as epiphanies, writers cherish that ecstatic transport of the soul because it propels their work.

The word "ecstasy" comes from the Greek word *Ekstasis*, meaning "to step outside oneself." This ecstatic moment is not so much mystical as dynamically charged, catapulting creative people into action that is richer and deeper than self-serving desires, pushing them through all the hard work of steady creation. The idea calls them out of themselves in that moment and extends an invitation that cannot be denied. I've learned that the ecstatic moment is the result of listening for a long time, like a birth that follows pregnancy. It seems to me that too many writers impatiently press toward birth; they lack the humility and patience required to listen while epiphany gestates.

LISTENING AND PRAYER

Prayer is the primary means by which we hear God's whispered inspiration. It is proof of a reverent and spiritually attentive heart. At its best, prayer is more than simply talking at God or even talking to God, it is talking with God. Prayer is communion with him. Dare I say it is fellowship and friendship, too? Conversation with God is the advance work you need to sustain a writing life and to buoy your heart. Make it your ambition, then, to pray a bit more frequently and thoughtfully every week. You will see the fruit in your spirit and in your work. You will undoubtedly find that the quality of your writing will mirror the depth and tone of your prayer life.

Frances Havergal, the hymn writer, once said, "Writing is praying with me, for I never seem to write even a verse by myself and feel like a little child writing what is dictated." She told a friend, "The Master has not put a chest of poetic gold into my possession and said, 'Now use it as you like!' but He keeps the gold and gives it to me piece by piece just when He will and as much as He will and no more." You can appreciate her feeling, her sense of smallness. That is how most writers feel. They know well and good that any generative success they experience owes more to God's generosity than to their dynamic personality or skills. That is another reason why generative writers listen to God. That is why they pray.

And this is how they pray: "Speak, therefore, Lord, for your servant listens. Thou hast the words of eternal life. Speak to me for the comfort of my soul and for the amendment of my life, for your praise, your glory, and your everlasting honor" (Thomas à Kempis, *The Imitation of Christ*).

BENEDICTION

May you seek God in the quiet moments and the chaotic ones. May you find in him a well of inspiration. May you incline your heart's ear toward God prayerfully, earnestly, simply, devotedly. May you listen for God's voice like one who drops a stone down a dark abyss, your senses strained keenly to hear the moment it hits water. May you cultivate your hearing so that he may clarify your life.

BALLAST

"The world you steer through is full of rocks, and shoals, and sandbanks. You are not sufficiently familiar with either lighthouses or charts. . . . You are in need of ballast."
—J. C. Ryle

The canoe was built for two, maybe three. We decided to take four. I climbed in the front, my friend sat on the curved floor, his dad sat in the rear, and their enormous dog joined us. In early April, the river ran high with snowmelt from the mountains. It was a formula for disaster, but we were veterans and much too self-assured.

We had canoed ten minutes of a forty-minute ride when we swept around a bend and disaster struck. The dog leapt to peer over the side and tore free from my friend's grip. Distracted by the dog now leaning on the edge of the canoe, my friend's dad and I stopped steering. By the time we noticed that we were careening into a giant thorn bush growing out of the river bank, it was too late. Our weight was too high in the boat and we all realized at the same time that we were about to tip over into the icy river.

Time froze for me. I saw my friend's dad drop his paddle and intentionally back flip out of his seat. As I watched him disappear into the churning water, I realized we had missed the thorn bush entirely. He had leapt at such an angle that his calculated shove pushed us back into the middle of the river. The loss of his top-heavy weight also meant we had enough ballast to keep us balanced.

Ballast. Such a necessity for safe travel, but so easily forgotten. We turned the canoe around and picked up my friend's dad. He climbed in dripping wet and chilled. The remainder of the ride was no pleasure cruise. We paddled sternly, silently, swiftly.

There's a lesson for writers in that story.

EVERY LIVING PERSON IS A PERSON OF FAITH

We each need ballast in our own boats, too. Though I've been using the mountain metaphor to describe our faith journey, I want to briefly change images. The soul is not only a traveler climbing a mountain, it is also a mighty ship sailing eternal seas. Mysterious winds drive it ever onward. Towering waves batter its flanks. It matters very much who stands at the helm, hands firmly upon the wheel. It matters who is bailing out water and loading ballast. If not God, then whom?

Regardless, the soul plunges forward, searching for something in which to believe. Every living person is a person of faith. Our faiths differ widely and some believe unconsciously in something they cannot name, but it is faith nonetheless. It is the filter for our perception and it compels us to action.

An atheist assumes certain things about reality because of his faith in a God-less world. Those assumptions dictate how he processes what he learns and how he decides right from wrong. A Christian like C. S. Lewis, on the other hand, holds certain assumptions about reality because of his faith in a God-filled world. Lewis said that his belief in God was like his belief that the sun has risen, not only because he could see it, but because by the sun he could see everything else.

Every single one of us lives by metaphysical assumptions that we hope sustain us during difficulties. Some of those assumptions prove to be more effective than others, but every soul needs a stabilizer to survive turbulent times. Self-fulfillment and the pursuit of happiness are not weighty enough. The only sufficient weight can be found in Scripture and in the Christian practices. These are our heritage—the Bible, the creeds, the church calendar, the doctrines of the church, and worship liturgies. These are tangible shapers of our perception and intuition. These give the heart, soul, and mind the weight needed to weather life's many storms.

My orientation toward God and intimacy with him is shaped by these things. They have a direct impact upon my day-to-day life. Indeed, the fervency of my writing invariably mirrors my faith's fervency. That is why reading theology, attending weekly worship, and conforming my life more and more to the rhythms of worship are so important. They give me a larger perspective while anchoring my restless heart and mind.

BALLAST FOUND IN DOCTRINES OF FAITH

That restlessness prompts many "Why?" questions in my life. The older Christian faith traditions have offered me a vision for hope, a larger story—a meta-narrative—that explains the why. They provide the story that settles me and broadens my view. God is the central character of that story, *not me*. He is the one who came as an infant to save mankind from the dragon, liberating us to follow God into a new promised land. This larger story acts as a filter through which we view everything, for it determines our decisions both great and small.

Christians believe the story is true, they believe it matters, and they believe it's a continuous and expanding narrative. Every theological book ever written explores some aspect of that narrative. Christian writers—no matter their field—invite others into the story, reinforce the story, and highlight the story because they know how meaningless life is without it.

BALLAST FOUND IN LITURGIES OF FAITH

But the meta-narrative provided by the Christian faith is not enough stabilization on its own. A buffeted soul also needs muscle-memory practices. The liturgies of the church serve as those practices. Some churches follow an age-old liturgical pattern—call to worship, confession, consecration, communion, and commission—that trains the heart and mind to think God's thoughts after him, to see as he sees.

Formal liturgies feel foreign to many, but every religious gathering has them, even those who boast in having none. In a world that promulgates isolation and self-reliance, formal liturgies give tangible reminders that God summons his people, God cleanses his people, God transforms his people, God feeds his people, and God sends his people. These are the easily-overlooked practices that train godly vision and that put weight in a writer's soul. These are the predictable routines that point to an unchanging God.

PURSUING GOD INSTEAD OF SELF-REALIZATION

Without ballast, we will drift into self-fulfillment and self-reliance every time. We quickly forget that only God can satisfy the human soul because we care more for the self than for the soul—and it doesn't help that we often confuse the two.

The self is certainly similar to the soul, but with all the longings for God and for righteousness removed. I think it was Eugene Peterson who called this preoccupation with self an "unGodded life" and grieved the loss. Generative writers aim to enrich and clarify the soul—their own souls and the souls of others. They seek wholeness in God, not simply self-fulfillment, psychological well-being, or self-reliance.

Jesus' repeated refrain is an encouragement to let go of self, to embark on a journey where dependence upon God outstrips self-reliance. Jesus tells his followers to see themselves as servants of the high king—regardless of circumstances—and to give themselves away rather than cherish their personal preciousness. So let it be with you. Founding your identity in God is necessary ballast for life.

Your baptism is a sacramental expression of this reality. In baptism, the child of God dies to sin, to self, and to the world, and is radically raised with Christ. Baptism marks us as God's, not our own, and this fact frees us from the chains of self-absorption.

But what happens if we forget our baptism or never get baptized at all? The changes in us are subtle. The heart drifts, focusing inward rather than upward, toward God. A selfish lean slowly turns us into misers of time, energy, projects, and money. The result is complacency, self-pity, torpor, diffidence, and abstruseness. It also results in the "smallification" of a life. I've fought that smallification with tooth and nail in my own life because selfishness and creativity are incompatible. So I'm learning to load ballast in the boat and pursue satisfaction with God. I'm trying.

PURSUING SHALOM INSTEAD OF HAPPINESS

Simone Weil believed that love is a direction, an inclination toward fulfillment. Sin's greatest corruption is in the heart's leaning. Instead of inclining toward God, our heart leans toward itself, toward self-satisfaction. Instead of inclining toward God's peace, we look for anything else that promises to end our wars—internal and external.

I once heard it said that all the world's experiments in happiness and power are simply humanity's effort to find shalom. "Shalom" is a Hebrew word that means God's peace, found in completeness or wholeness. It's a fullness that encourages us to give. It's not the same as mere happiness—being cheerful or in good spirits. Let's not confuse them, otherwise we'll grow easily discouraged.

Shalom is an abiding rest and flourishing peace with God, not simply an absence of war. In fact, happiness is not a condition for shalom at all, nor is tolerance or niceness. It can come by generosity, kindness, and service, but shalom is also found in breaking down towers (Judg. 8:9) and in punishment (Isa. 53:5). None of these are easy and none of them qualify as happy times, but happiness is never the goal. Shalom is.

Generative writers are agents of shalom. They have a divine opportunity to creatively respond to fragmentation and disintegration in society without stooping to sermonizing or giving in to the tidal wave of futility and hopelessness inherent in people who have rejected God. They expose the shallow desires that drive the world while enriching their readers with something more substantive.

Modern civilization is a thin film veiling an abyss of chaos and rage and shame. Generative writers tear holes in the veil and reveal our need for God. In our desperation, who will lead us to the only One who can fill our need for real peace, if not writers like you? In our loneliness and alienation, who will show us the face of God, if not you? The world is full of people careening in the dark. Who will give them back their sun?

You and I have a unique opportunity to unveil God to a disenchanted people. We get to speak into others' pain, to remind them of their humanity, to cut through tribal rhetoric in a way that clear, logical expressions of truth cannot. Where the discourse of violence has severed relationships and made healing nearly impossible in a family or in a neighborhood or across racial lines, generative writers can speak and, by God's grace, be heard. We get to share our ballast with others. We get to give them God and thereby restore to them their humanity. All acts of love—especially writing—have this fundamental purpose.

PURSUING A DIVINE PERSPECTIVE INSTEAD OF A MORTAL PERSPECTIVE

When we seek God rather than self, when we seek shalom rather than happiness, and when we seek a divine perspective rather than a mortal one, we travel the ancient roads God calls us to walk in the book of Jeremiah: "Stand in the ways and see, and ask for the old paths, where the good way is, and walk in it; then you will find rest for your souls" (Jer. 6:16). The world is full of people who long to find the good way, but they seek it in all the wrong places and by all the wrong means. They don't like feeling unhinged, restless, but they don't know what else to do.

Work tirelessly to point the world back to the ancient ways—back to the well-worn, narrow footpath where shalom is found for the soul. Your faith gives you eyes to see. Continue Christ's work by helping others to see.

BENEDICTION

May you sail life's stormy seas in a well-built ship with strong ballast. In all the turbulence—the wind and waves that buffet your boat—may you find satisfaction with God, taste his shalom, and discover a divine vantage point.

CONDUITS OF LIFE

"All men know that the true good is Happiness, and all men seek it, but for the most part by wrong routes—like a drunk man who knows he has a house but can't find his way home."
—Chaucer, "The Knight's Tale"

My Uncle Gary was not only a man of God, he was a top-tier engineer. A water man. He spent thirty-six years of his life supplying water to the nearly half-a-million people living in Colorado Springs and many more in that part of the state. He knew those mountains, each and every landmark, each and every stream. He was the one responsible for a decade-long project that provided water from the Arkansas river through ninety-inch diameter pipes and stored it in massive underground tanks for times of drought that often cripple the area—a project $825 million in the making. His cutting edge engineering feats can still be found throughout the state.

He was a water man whose last name means "camped by the

waters." How fitting that they found his body in a stream. He was riding his bike on a trail when he suffered a heart attack that, as far as they could tell, killed him instantly, pitching him off the bike and down into the water. In honor of his service to the state, Colorado is naming a massive new reservoir and recreational area after him. Even in death, his name will be connected to water, to life.

BIOS VS. ZOE

The parallels between the generative life and Gary's life are readily evident. While his concern was with the literal water and the literal life of people, your concern is with the metaphorical water and spiritual vigor of others. His, with *bios* (Greek for physical life); yours, with *zoe* (Greek for spiritual life). *Bios* is nurtured by food, water, and oxygen. Their corollaries in *zoe* are the Scriptures (food), the Sacraments (water), and prayer (oxygen). Your great concern and the deep lean of your life is *zoe*.

People seek physical and spiritual satisfaction, but our search for spiritual satisfaction, our heart's thirst, dictates what we do with the body and how we try to satisfy the heart. We often do anything in our power to satisfy *bios* in a misguided attempt to satisfy *zoe's* ache.

WE SEEK WHAT CAN NEVER SATISFY

Augustine said that our main problem is not that we hate rather than love, but that our loves are misplaced and wrongly ordered.

He meant that we not only love the wrong things, but also that our loves are prioritized poorly. Like a drunk who spends his money on alcohol rather than food and water, we spend our emotional and physical energy on what cannot ultimately satisfy. Material things—food, sex, travel, friendship, work, drugs, shopping—can only satisfy temporarily because they were not made to satisfy the eternal longing of the heart. Only God can fully satisfy. Material things lack the width and height, the necessary proportion, to fit immortal souls.

In Isaiah 55:2, God asks his people how they came to prioritize their loves so poorly. Why do they spend themselves on what cannot meet their true needs? "Come to the waters!" he cries. "Why do you spend money for what is not bread, and your wages for what does not satisfy? Listen carefully to me, and eat what is good, and let your soul delight itself in abundance. Incline your ear, and come to me. Hear, and your soul shall live" (Isa. 55:1-3). Did you catch that? Incline. Satisfaction begins by leaning into God. A redeemed heart seeks satisfaction in God, an unredeemed heart seeks satisfaction in itself. Writers cannot offer *zoe* to others when they are not fed by it themselves.

EPEKTASIS AND IMMERSION IN GOD

Our ability to serve as a conduit of *zoe* depends upon our inner orientation, what Gregory of Nyssa called *epektasis*, literally "tension towards" or a stretching forward to the divine. This *epektasis* is difficult to describe and to enflesh, impossible to describe syllogistically. It can only be hinted at in poetry and story and song. One of the many gifts my parents gave me—and we have tried to give to you—was a storied imagination, the necessary equipment for navigating what others have hinted at since men and women starting using words to explore and explain their own existence—all the enigmatic nuance and mystery of this mortal journey and God's relationship to it.

True, Christianity is not strictly a mystery religion—the Apostle's Creed is simple and clear enough—but the Christian religion overflows with mysteries. Generative writers stand in the overflow and stretch their souls' nerve endings to feel the coolness of the water that is God.

On my own journey of faith, I've found it difficult to remember the difference between immersion and grasping. I've seen some people immerse themselves in God while others try to catch him. Some have made faith a matter of the heart's lean. Others have made it a matter of willpower and piety. These observations have convinced me that the quality of our spiritual water declines when we turn the spiritual life into a series of checklists instead of letting godward desires flood life and seep into every corner.

The Bible promises that if we search for God with all our hearts, then we shall find him (Jer. 29:13, Deut. 4:29), but this searching implies not so much willpower as an orientation, a pressing toward God with the desires. Certainly not a checklist of holy actions.

God reminds us to meditate on his words day and night (Ps. 1:2, Josh. 1:8) and this constant contact with God is what promises great reward. Faith is not merely an intellectual affair; it is the whole person's encounter with the hidden God, requiring an engagement of the mind, the heart, the will, the body, the imagination, and the soul. And if Hans Urs von Balthasar is correct in saying that only God can recognize God—we're too mortal and too corrupted by sin—then faith is, in a sense, God in us recognizing himself and inclining us toward himself. So we start with listening, leaning, meditating day and night; holy living will follow.

Generative writers try to drink from God's word every day (Ps. 119:97)—it need not be in great quantities. Doing so nourishes their work from underground, like a subterranean spring. In John 4:13-14, Jesus says to the adulterer at the well, "Whoever drinks of this water will thirst again, but whoever drinks of the water that I shall give him will never thirst. But the water that I shall give him will become in him a fountain of water springing up into everlasting life." When writers are subsumed by Christ, their work takes on a greater degree of complexity, a richer texture, and a deeper beauty—a cup of cool water pointing to the Fount of Living Water. So writers drink faithfully, even if only in small, regular sips.

STUDY YOURSELF AND EVALUATE YOUR DESIRES

We best serve others by learning about ourselves. Knowing our own hearts helps us understand other hearts better. When we learn what helps our spiritual engines run smoothly, we can help other people struggling with their engine problems. A man who does not know his car will not know how to fix it when something in the engine goes haywire, but the man who has worked to become familiar with the car's inner workings is better able to fix it. Likewise, your heart is a highly-tuned instrument and it will serve you well to know it so that you can know what is the matter when it is out of tune.

You will soon discover that your heart is often out of tune, its desires disordered. Go to God with these things. He knows your heart better than you know it. Learn your heart's tendencies, its fears, its predilections, its propensities, its true desires (as opposed to the ones you know you ought to have). Study your heart when it undergoes pressures of various kinds and you will learn, over time, where it errs and where it stays true.

You live and work with people of various convictions, some of whom believe one of two false views of the person. The first view is that human beings are primarily rational, processing information and making conscious decisions. The second view is that people are primarily emotional, responding to circumstances instinctively and passionately.

As you know, these views are incomplete. They indicate a false dichotomy. God has given us intellect, heart, will, imagination, and senses. They work together to help us navigate the world, and God uses them together to draw us to himself. You will be tempted to understand yourself and others compartmentally rather than holistically, but unnecessarily so. Recognize these diverse faculties, these remarkable gifts, and give them their due respect. They are deeply intertwined with the heart's desires.

Descartes famously said, "I think, therefore I am" and, as James K. A. Smith observes, a philosophy like that implies an intellectual deliberateness not really seen in reality (*You Are What You Love*). We're not logical machines always making the best possible decisions given adequate information, acting only after we consider our options. While sometimes true, many of our decisions are actually unconscious, tuned by the heart's desire. The heart's desires color how we think and propel us to action. We're not fundamentally knowers or even believers, we're lovers.

I think that is one reason why Jesus told stories, why he asked "What do you seek?" (John 1:38). Those who can answer that ultimate question can identify their souls' thirsts. They can better understand their choices and better see where they are going. Generative people ask similar questions of themselves and others.

If you would be like them, learn to evaluate your heart's longings. Many of us come to realize that we're spiritual and emotional infants whose petty desires are narrow and immediate rather than expansive and eternal. Our moral failure is not the result of character weakness as much as it is the result of small ideals, tiny and ill-ordered loves.

These are not insignificant matters. Since we're writers, what we feed ourselves we pass on to others. What we read matters. What we listen to matters. What we watch matters. Where we go matters. Whomever we choose as a friend matters. Whether we regularly read God's word matters. How we participate in the sacraments and how we pray matters.

Our human appetites—for relationship, for pleasure, for happiness—affect our spiritual hearing and seeing, our creating and speaking. For this reason Proverbs 4:23 says, "Keep your heart with all diligence, for out of it spring the issues of life." These "issues of life" are a person's habits and immersions. Be aware, therefore, of your immersions.

SNAKES IN THE WELL

The small community in which I grew up shared one water well. I never remember it going dry. In fact, I never gave it much thought until a man came running to inform my dad that there were snakes in the well. By the time we arrived, many folks had gathered around. It was a covered well so I could not look inside, but the nest of snakes was already confirmed. I remember the panic surging inside my little heart at the thought of a dozen dark, poisonous serpents lurking at the source of our water. As I recall, they drove the snakes out at great personal risk. Thankfully, we never lost use of our water source. I was young and this memory is rather foggy, but this event has remained with me as a fitting metaphor for the small distractions and addictions that can sneak into one's heart and endanger the whole person.

LEARNING TO SEE THE IRONIES OF FAITH

Your ability to serve as an effective conduit depends upon your ability to see people as God sees us. He knows that we have snakes in our well, but that never seems to cause him hesitation. He seems more interested in narrative possibility than in narrative probability. In other words, he's more interested in the what-ifs that no one sees coming.

God's story as told through the Christian narrative offers us new eyes. It suggests purpose where we only see pain, gladness where we expect grief, resurrection where we experience only death. God seems to say, "Look for unexpected moments. Look for ironies, incongruities between what is expected and what actually happens." We expect the strength of evil and pride to win, but they lead only to death. We expect almighty God to enter his creation as a caesar, overthrowing his enemies by sheer power, but he comes as an infant born to obscure parents in a forgotten part of the world. We expect glory to come by way of domination, not by way of servanthood.

In God's story, the child becomes the teacher, the saviors are the lowly, and the saved are not always whom we expect. Furthermore, the haven is found in the storm, the lame enter Heaven first, and the strong man dies to rescue the weak. Irony of ironies, even he who hates God most can be made "the unwilling instrument of grace" (Flannery O'Connor), doing most of the spade work necessary for the seed of grace to sprout into redemption. Learn to see with eyes of faith. Embrace such ironies.

OBSERVE PEOPLE, WALK IN THEIR SHOES

God is not deceived by externals. He knows each person's inner attic and cellar. He sees where we hide our scuttling-cockroach desires and where we lock our secrets. He knows what small gesture will reveal our deepest fears. He knows with equal intimacy those who love him and those who hate him. He knows that every devil of a man had a mother, feels self-justified, remembers his failures more than his victories, and considers himself perfectly sane. Like the rest of us.

Observe people in the particulars with faith-infused eyes. If you would be a good conduit of life, recognize that people are more complex than they appear. At our core, we're bumbling burglars of the divine mansion, who would rather take by force than accept what has been given to us freely. And yet we are, and ever will be, immortal diamonds made in the image of God.

So, generously observe people, learn to walk around in their shoes. Learn to see with their eyes, listen with their ears. Listen to the soul behind their words, observe their spirit behind its form. Does a man bristle, lash out, curmudgeonly hurl himself against those nearest to him like a grizzly bear? Perhaps he is deeply anxious. Is she brash, recalcitrant, always posturing for praise? Perhaps she carries a great burden of shame and does not know what to do with it. Be concerned with the spiritual poverties that they hold in common with everyone. Be acquainted with their limitations, their deepest failures. Nurture an empathy for others because you know the God who made them as he made you.

As a writer, you're especially called to love people. Banality, indifference, contempt, rage, and vapid thinking in others will make them difficult to love until you realize that those expressions mask eternal longing, deep loss, unquenched thirst, and gnawing hunger for something transcendent, lasting, and real: a God hunger. We often do not know what this hunger is for and so we fling out, sometimes violently, in search of something to satisfy it. And when our tiny loves go unsatisfied (as they must for people untethered from their maker), we bemoan our lot and rage against the stars.

God knows we're haunted by the shadow of a meaning much larger than ourselves, a shadow that dogs us from behind, dodging from tree to tree (Flannery O'Connor). Let that image inform your writing—whether poetry, stories, or essays. Learn to love people with a tough-minded soberness that gladly anticipates God's redemptive work in their lives as he has worked in yours and this, too, will make you a better conduit of life. Give us life! And give it to us in all its diverse particularity.

BENEDICTION

When you feel ill-equipped to see people the way God sees them, to depict them honestly and honorably, to give people life, may God replenish you with the gift of faith. Your gait up this mountain will not always be a steady one. Sometimes your faith will feel strong, but sometimes your faith will be nothing more than a whispered "Yes," barely an exhale. This, too, is faith and should be counted as such, however small. It is divine *zoe*, much needed refreshment in a parched world. Irenaeus once said, "The glory of God is a human being fully alive." May you live so that others may have life. Now to God who works powerfully within us, to him be glory (Eph. 3:20-21).

CONTENTMENT AND AMBITION

"Things have value in exact proportion to what they cost."
—A. G. Sertillanges, *The Intellectual Life*

I once attended a concert at which the opening act had clearly resigned himself to being an opening act. His voice was unnoteworthy, and his poetry was mediocre, but the man could certainly play the guitar. I was mesmerized. Or, I should say, I would have been mesmerized had he not acted overly thankful and fortunate to just be there. His self-deprecatory comments about his poor story-telling and his off-handed remarks about *if* we wanted to buy his music and *if* he someday wrote some new songs diluted the entire experience.

He had clearly worked hard to learn the guitar. And I have no doubt that if he had walked on that stage as if he were the main event and played with that kind of joy and authority, he would soon have been a main event somewhere, or at least joined with a band, a creative community where his gifts could thrive. As it stands, his gifts appear to have no trajectory. God made him to play the guitar, but this young artist did not carry himself with joyful confidence because he had not given his talent direction.

I don't know his story. Maybe his ambition met the wall of failure so many times that he lost heart. Maybe he had practiced self-deprecation for so many years that he could see nothing but failure now. I suspect, though, that he simply didn't know how to ambitiously pursue his art while simultaneously being content with where he was in the process. If so, his struggle is common. Writers, especially, have difficulty being content and working ambitiously. I certainly share that struggle.

ACHIEVEMENT VS. FAME

I once believed ambition and contentment were antithetical, so I swung between the two. I later learned that if everyone had to set aside ambition in order to attain contentment, nobody would accomplish anything in the world. Generative writers should be ambitious, chasing the next project, perfecting their skills, reading avidly, learning how to be more effective in their vocation, but their ambition cannot be for fame. God prohibits vainglorious pursuits. And the pursuit of fame erodes the godly character necessary for generative work.

Desire achievement, not fame. Desire vision, not noto-riety. Desire a chance to enrich the world, not a chance to be well-known in it. None of what I've said in these letters should preclude a strong work ethic, a determined aim, nor a longing to be the best at what you do. The legendary George Pocock, who built some of the best rowing shells of his time, once feared that he would become a second-rate artisan if he sold his stock and became wealthy. He preferred first-class craftsmanship and relative poverty to losing his incentive on a golden couch.

He was a confident man and we can attain a similar confidence in due time if we desire to transcend the mire of mediocrity while steering clear of the easy life. Champions are made by the resistance they overcome. That applies as much to generative living as it does to business or sports. This championship caliber is achievable with a steady, humble trust in God and simultaneously a steady and humble work ethic.

SEEK GOD'S KINGDOM, NOT YOUR OWN

People tend to process their life experience through two filters: power and competition. As I heard someone once say, "Life is competition." His mindset was more capitalist than Christian and I don't agree with it. I don't think scripture does either, but writers like me are especially susceptible to this mindset. We can easily view the writing life like we view most vocations, characterized by ladder climbing, greed, and political power plays. We pine over our level of income and the degree of fame other authors enjoy.

The temptation to make a name for oneself is an ancient one. Satan used the rhetoric of self-aggrandizement to lure

Jesus in the desert. Christ resisted the temptation. He remained humble and, therefore, content. He helps us live the same way.

I'm convinced that our spiritual health depends upon humility, especially for writers. When we're humble, we navigate the world more easily, ask better questions, learn more, feel less pressure to perform, and get along better in community. In fact, when we're humble, we're more generative. Unfortunately, pride's subtleties and the fact that we write for an audience make it difficult to remain humble over long periods of time. The subtle shift from a generative lean to a marketing lean is easy. Without constraint, love gradually shifts inward.

St. John of the Cross once wrote, "At the evening of our day, we will be judged by our loving." Have we loved God's fame or our own? Will the paper trail of our life lead to the kingdom of God or will it lead to a personal kingdom? Will it reveal a life spent in patient, determined, purposeful pursuit of God and his kingdom, or will it reveal a life spent in the pursuit of self-aggrandizement? The answers to those questions dictate how we use our time, our money, and our energy.

A VIADUCT OF GOD'S GRACE

Truly, God loves his children. We are, indeed, precious in his sight, but it is not our preciousness that matters. God matters. In the end, we're just a viaduct of God's grace and truth and beauty. The invention of the viaduct was an important gift to mankind, but no right-minded person cares more for the viaduct than for the life-giving water it carries. The truth of the matter is that we're not all that important in the grand scheme of things. We're just conduits. O, the liberty of that thought!

Jesus said, "Blessed are the meek, for they shall inherit the earth." Becoming a conduit requires a kind of dying to self, and dying to self requires meekness. Asking others for wisdom requires meekness. Seeing sacramentally requires meekness. Imitating others in little things requires meekness. We cannot give the world back to God renewed, relit, and retuned unless we live as though he has given it to us. Our meekness is the key to this inheritance and, therefore, key to our lasting impact.

Humility, not pride, is the prerequisite for lasting shalom, peace with God. Faithfulness, not fame, is the pathway to lasting gladness. Indeed, blessed are the poor in spirit. Such is the promise of a God who humbled himself for our joy and for his glory. Writers who aim for humility usually find contentment along the way, while those who aim for fame rarely do.

Humility is the hallmark of greatness, and contentment is its reward.

CONTENTMENT IS THE FRAME OF YOUR HOUSE

True contentment is a life-long study and absolutely unattainable to those who think that the heart's satisfaction hinges on external circumstances. True contentment, true gratification is a disposition not impacted by storms nor by sunny skies. It is the heart's frame and, like a well-built house, depends upon the builder's faithful craftsmanship. As you build the house of your heart, a house that will remain your home for eternity and will be the wellspring of your writing, pay attention to its foundation and to its main support beams.

THE FIGHT FOR CONTENTMENT

When we spoke on the phone the other night, your voice evinced a kind of certitude and calm in your soul. I sensed no hurry. No distraction. No agitation. We were just together in the moment, awake in the darkness, talking across the distance. That kind of peace is never a constant in our broken world—as you well know—but it is a gift and it is a gift that comes more often to those whose lives are built for peace, to those who have cultivated contentment. You build your life for peace by practicing contentment, even by fighting for it.

Fighting for contentment involves a lot of fellowship with God, of course, but it requires boundaries that guard the heart against discontentment. For example, it doesn't take long for my heart to grow discontent with my car, my clothing, and my body when I marinate in so many advertisements during televised football games, so I need to limit my exposure to those advertisements. I grow discontent with my home when I thumb through realty and home improvement magazines, so I limit my exposure to those as well.

The fight for contentment, like the fight for joy, is never finished and never stays won. As those you most love and respect have exhibited—especially your grandparents—contentment does not depend upon having more, being more, or knowing more; it does not depend upon being somewhere else or being with someone else. Lasting contentment is found in communion with God regardless of circumstances.

In 1 Timothy 6, Christians are charged to be content with the food and clothing they have. Paul even seems to imply that godliness is not found apart from contentment: "Godliness with contentment is great gain. For we brought nothing into this world, and it is certain we can carry nothing out. And having food and clothing, with these we shall be content" (v. 6-8). And the writer of Hebrews reminds us to keep covetousness out of our conversations—even our thought patterns—to be content with what we have since Christ has promised to fill our greatest need. Since he will never leave nor forsake us (Heb. 13:5), we need not be restless in this existentially restless world.

THE CALL TO GREATNESS

Nevertheless, you may sometimes feel a subterranean potential and a call to greatness that is hard to describe, but very real. You're not alone in feeling that way. Some might suggest you ignore that call as nothing but the urge of your personal pride. Perhaps it is nothing but pride, but I would not easily discount it if I were you. Yes, it is a kind of restlessness, but it is still compatible with contentment. This urge to do something important is not at all antithetical to the generative life.

It is entirely possible to write and pursue greatness, but the generative life puts the brakes on an egomaniacal pursuit. The generative life directs the pursuit of greatness, making that greatness less about personal power and more about generosity; less about self-aggrandizement and more about broadening impact; less about self-promotion and more about sharing the Good News. It imitates Christ who set aside his heavenly glory to become a human being for the sake of all people. Greatness for Christian writers looks like extravagant self-sacrifice. It also looks like a humble recognition and thankfulness for the gifts God has given to us.

The subterranean urge to be great comes to those who know that they are good at something. When asked why she wrote, Flannery O'Connor once said, "Because I'm good at it." Her response might sound a bit egotistical to a people accustomed to false humility, but we will never amount to anything in any field if we cannot answer, "Because I'm good at it." Yes, we will have to do many things in life that we're not good at, and we should do those things; but if we're good at something, then humility demands that we acknowledge that fact, certainly in our heart.

Like the parts of a body, each person is equipped to do some things well and not others. The hand does not think, nor does the ear speak. If healthy, they do what they were made to do and do it to the best of their ability. Some people do what they were made to do and receive great fame while others use their gifts and remain obscure. What matters is the effective use of those gifts, not the fame. Glory belongs to God and he dispenses it liberally, as he so desires.

HANDLING PRAISE

When I get the opportunity to speak with someone I consider famous, I often ask how he or she guards against the negative effects of fame and glory. Fernando Ortega, the modern psalmist, told me that those who know him best keep him safeguarded from listening to the fickle praise of the public. He encouraged me to keep wrestling against the pull of inflated ego because the first sign that you have fallen prey to ambition and fame is that you stop being wary.

In a different conversation, a world-renowned speaker and writer told me that he allows himself twenty-four hours to enjoy an award before stuffing it in a bottom drawer in his filing cabinet and moving on. He said that if he lingers upon them too long, awards and fame tempt him to stop plowing in hope. In moderation, praise fans the flame of creativity and work, but too much snuffs it out.

Learning from those who have faced issues you have yet to encounter is an important means of gaining wisdom. Proverbs 4:7 exhorts us to seek wisdom because it "is the principle thing; therefore get wisdom. And in all your getting, get understanding. Exalt her, and she will promote you; she will bring you honor, when you embrace her." The pursuit of wisdom will keep you focused on true glory given by God to his faithful ones, rather than distracted by the fool's gold of false acclaim.

Remember the Pharisees who did whatever it took to make sure people knew just how pious they were? They got attention and even a measure of fame, but Christ said that they already had their reward and would not get God's praise (Matt. 6:1–4).

Christ encourages us to be different and reminds us that the works we do in obscurity are seen by God and will be rewarded by him. Keep this lesson in mind when you start pining for attention, longing for fame and glory.

Fame and glory are not synonymous in God's economy: the greatest glory is usually found in obscurity. Perhaps your exaltation will take the form of fame and praise, but it might look entirely different. It might be something deeper and longer-lasting and less measurable, like loyalty or like love. The loyalty and love of one reader is gift enough.

No matter the size of your audience, write well. Mediocrity will be a significant threat to your effectiveness. The mediocre, or writers in danger of becoming mediocre, are often pretentious, claiming to be great, but the truly great are not interested in trite estimations of their work. The truly great are hunters, chasing achievement rather than fame. They are craftsmen, unchanged by fame or anonymity.

HORSES AND CHARIOTS

Perhaps God intends to give you many hundreds of loyal and loving readers. How does that happen? An old adage says that

God helps those who help themselves. Sounds pious enough, but it is a subtle corruption of the truth. Christians are called to serve others and trust God to bless that service, however he will.

We are in the hands of God and the outcome of our effort is entirely up to him. Neither horses nor chariots will save us—only God can do that (Ps. 20:7, Ps. 44:6)—but God often uses horses and chariots to bring about his victories. We use the tools God has given us, like sound business principles and technology, to advance his important work. These tools can help us serve more effectively, but they can easily become the principal thing instead of reliance on God.

SIMPLIFY YOUR NEEDS

When I was your age, a paralyzing panic set in every time I thought of the five billion people in the world who, I imagined, had to shoulder and jostle their way into some kind of purpose and identity. The thought would stop me in my tracks, right on the sidewalk, and I wondered how I would ever out-hustle the rest. Nobody had yet told me so baldly that "life is competition," but I would have been unravelled if they had. How was I—little ol' me with skinny arms and sluggish brain—supposed to compete with all those people? It did not help that I grew up, like you, in a marketed world where billboards interrupted every view of the horizon, and advertisements interrupted every television show.

We have been catechized by slogans and indoctrinated by marketing teams to beat the best and be the best. If we're not ahead of the capitalist curve then apparently we should be worried. Some anxieties are helpful motivators to action, but I've never found that kind of existential pressure very useful.

At my age, those worries have not disappeared entirely, but I suppress them whenever they surface. Instead, I remind myself to lead a quiet life, to mind my own business, and to work with my hands (1 Thess. 4:11). Discontented people feel pressured to be someone special and do something extraordinary, but content people do the next thing—no matter how menial.

Discontentment balloons our felt needs, but contentment recognizes reality. I try to remind myself of how little I am, how little is required of me, and how little I actually need. I'm not a major player in the geopolitical landscape. I'm not a significant historical figure. What is required of me in life? That I love mercy, do justly, and walk humbly with God (Mic. 6:8). And what do I need? Food (just enough), shelter, and friendship. I imagine that you and I could survive on a diet of shortbread, cheese, and raisins.

And what if we do not get the acclaim or the dream job or the model home? We have these friends now. We have this roof and these insulated walls. So what if the cupboards are a little sparse? We have far more than shortbread, cheese, and raisins. Best of all, we have God's promise that, even to old age, he will carry us! He has made you and me and he hears our cries (Isa. 46:4).

RIDING THE TENSION

Your ability to ride the tension between ambition and contentment, between glory and obscurity, should never get easy. All your life, step to the rhythm of humble gratefulness for the small things. As you keep moving, God gives grace for each moment. Use the grace given.

Your survival (and I mean that quite literally) depends upon your ability to simultaneously embrace the urge to be great while recognizing your insignificance. History is littered with people who lost their bearings and sometimes lost their lives because they could not hold those in tension.

God faithfully gives us reality checks, reminders that we're dependent upon him, that our horses and chariots have serious limitations. These reality checks help us see our place in the grand scheme of things. We're simply God's tool. Cling to humility and self-forgetfulness in your pursuit of achievement. Keep selfish ambition at bay, but press ahead with writing and generative reach.

Life is not all about us. You and I are neither the star, nor the center. And the point of life is not our glory, our work, or our fame, but God's. Let us be content, seeking first God's kingdom, not our own, and with that single aim we will simplify the course of life. When we genuinely prioritize God's kingdom, everything else in life will be given its proper attention.

BENEDICTION

May you live patiently determined. May you chase achievement, not fame. May your heart find satisfaction with God and the strength to do your best work. May your life, dear one, be characterized by patient persistence.

TIME

"Become an open singing-bowl, whose chime
Is richness rising out of emptiness,
And timelessness resounding into time.

And when the heart is full of quietness
Begin the song exactly where you are."
                    —Malcolm Guite, from "Singing Bowl"

Many years ago, I visited England for ten days with your mother and a group of college students. We visited a lot of historical sites, one of which was going to be C. S. Lewis's house. The day we arrived in Oxford, however, a terrible sickness struck your mom. She could not travel. By the following morning, we knew she needed immediate treatment. I was unhappy, critical, and impatient. Of all the sites we'd visited, this was the one I most wanted to see. The tour group took off without us. I found a clinic's address.

While we waited for the bus, she commented on how the large, glass building a block away looked like a medical center. Nevertheless, we caught the bus and rode twenty minutes to the other side of Oxford. We found a piece of paper taped to the clinic's window: "We have moved." I wrote down the new address and we climbed aboard another bus. To our consternation, the bus delivered us to our starting point. The clinic? In the glass building. I didn't even try to hide my frustration.

We spent an hour or more at the clinic where your mother received treatment. All I could think about was what I was missing. When we got out, she asked if I wanted to take a walking tour of Lewis's life in Oxford. Of course I did.

Our first stop required a short bus ride. The map said we should take a right down the first street once we climbed off of the bus. So we started walking, looking carefully for any street and watching for street signs. We walked for a half-mile with no indication of either. I suggested that we turn around and call it a day, but she said we could keep trying. So we walked another half-mile before I decided to ask the next person we met for directions. To my massive disappointment, that person did not speak a lick of English. In Oxford, of all places, we found the only person who did not know English on a main road which was inexplicably empty of pedestrians. My anger boiled. We walked another few blocks before turning around, frustrated.

I fumed during the mile-long walk back to the bus until I saw a street sign. It was the street we had both missed. Neither of us saw it the first time.

The next hour or more, we wandered from landmark to landmark. We got lost at one point and, from pure exhaustion, decided to rest in a shaded cemetery couched in a neighborhood. As your mother rested, I walked the cemetery in search of any tombstone with a famous name. I thought it unlikely, but perhaps Lewis was buried there. I had no idea if he was, but I had nothing to do other than wait for your mother to rest.

"What are you looking for?" she asked.

"I'm looking for a vine. I know that a vine grows near his tombstone," I replied.

"Do you mean this vine?" she asked.

Surely not, I thought to myself. But there, not fifteen feet away, was a vine. Below it sat his tombstone. Once again, I had walked right past it. I wept, a result of happiness combined with fatigue and exasperation.

Rain threatened the remainder of our walk to Lewis's house. I knew that we would not get to see inside the house because tours are booked long in advance. Even our tour group had not scheduled a visit. They were just going to drive by and look at it. But as I approached, I remember praying that God would send a torrential downpour so that I could go to the house and ask if my sick wife and I could take refuge inside while it rained.

Yes, I was entirely selfish about the prayer, and God knew that. Even as I prayed, the clouds separated and the sun beat down upon us. My frustration at God reached new heights. Sweat dripped down my face just as we approached the house. I reached up to remove my Washington State University baseball cap. In the three seconds it took to remove my hat, the back door of Lewis's house opened. A man stepped out, glanced at us, and said, "Tell me you're from Washington State!"

"Yes we are," I replied, bewildered.

He energetically approached and explained that he was from the state of Washington too, that his daughter went to school on the west side of the state, and that he was part of a small group touring the house. There was plenty of room for us to join them for the tour and even get some food if we wanted. A wave of surprise, happiness, and relief washed over me, and with it, the realization of my day-long frustrations at God and at so many petty inconveniences. I felt so small, so ashamed. And then the dawning on my mind of all the detours and errors and delays necessary to orchestrate that three second encounter.

Three seconds of time.

I had felt the pressure of time all day long. Time wasted. Time lost. From the beginning, nothing seemed to be going my way, until those three seconds when I realized that everything had been moving toward this moment. That was no chance meeting. Everything had happened right on time.

We ate lunch with the group. We toured the house. I held Lewis's pipe in my hand. We met Walter Hooper, the man so instrumental in compiling Lewis's work. Gift upon gift upon gift. More than I could have dreamed or imagined. We later learned that our team of touring college students had run out of time to visit Lewis's house. They lacked the reservation necessary to go into his house and decided to skip it altogether.

ALL TIME IS GOD'S TIME

I learned a priceless lesson that day. "A man's heart plans his way, but the Lord directs his steps" (Prov. 16:9). I repented deep in my heart and thought, "Lord, not my will be done! Only yours, O Lord!" That day indelibly stamped upon my heart the truth that all time is God's time.

I write this letter on a sunny day when all seems right with the world, but I know that tomorrow will bring its own inconveniences, its own obstacles, its own small storms. Days hurtle by at increasingly higher speeds as I age. I feel the weight of time lost, and I feel the mysterious complications of living purposefully without any idea of how long I have left to live or to labor. Daily, I face the limitations of my plans and my remarkable impatience with time.

You are yet young, but I suspect that you feel the same weight and similar frustrations. Time, at least our view of it, exposes so much about us. That's why a real test of our faith and our purpose is in how we think about time and how we use it.

Time is a strange thing. It can expand and shrink and slow down and speed up and theoretically even bend, but it all belongs to God. All time is God's time. Meekness stems from the recognition that we live at the crossroads of mortal time and God's time, God's space and our space. Somehow, some way, all the hustle and bustle of our trivial moments overlap with eternity. We live in the space between, this luminous and liminal space between God's promises and his provision that theologians call *kairos*, meaning, the pregnant moment.

KAIROS

God functions in *kairos*. From his perspective, functioning within a divine dimension, every moment of every day is *kairos*. Your effectiveness as a writer will depend upon your ability to fashion habits, perspectives, and hopes according to *kairos*. Just as you're called to be ambitious and content, so too are you called to press ahead and wait on God, to anticipate the completion of whatever you're doing while trusting God to help in the timing. This combination of trust and continued work is nothing short of miraculous; nevertheless, I encourage you to practice it and pray for it.

A friend of mine once said that life is a timed event with eternal consequences—death and eternity loom over all of us. This sobering recognition prompts many people to wrongly value quality time over quantity time when it comes to things like relationships. But relationships are built by lots of car rides in a blue Nissan truck.

Do you remember my old truck? The engine breakdowns? The times I tried to make it to the end of the month, but ran out of gas and we had to call your grandfather to save the day? Do you remember when I rear-ended that poor lady because you had just spilled your drink all over the seat? I told you many stories in that truck. We had a thousand hours of time together in that truck, back and forth from school, from the store, from basketball games.

Something inside you broke on the day I gave that old truck away. I don't think it was the truck you loved as much as it was what the truck represented. We didn't aim to make those thousand hours special. We didn't guard our time in that truck as if it were precious. It was entirely ordinary time full of unplanned conversations, silence, plastic seats, and interruptions. What turned out to be quality time was built out of quantity time.

The same holds true for writing. Quality writing is built out of quantity writing. Have no doubts, quantity writing simply takes time, so don't aim for long, uninterrupted writing sessions. Those are much too rare. Instead, take a little time every day to write. Let it happen in the flow of life.

THE ILLUSION OF "YOUR TIME"

Kairos time is where we live. There is no such thing as "my time." It's all God's. That realization prevents us from squandering time and it helps us view interruptions rightly. To those who aim for quality time over quantity time, interruptions will always be a major hassle. We function within God's time in a particular geographical and historical space, surrounded by particular people. Our God-given duty is to those people in that place and at that time. They are not barriers to generative living, but its aim. They do not impede creative, meaningful living, they feed it and receive it.

Much of my writing takes place at a desk that sits where life swirls around it, where children cannot go downstairs or up without passing nearby. Part of this setup was simply a necessity of space in a small house, but I've come to value the interruptions—most of the time. Undoubtedly, I will jump at the opportunity to have my own space if we move someday, but even then I hope to remember the value of interruptions and the duty of serving. If you remember that you labor miraculously in *kairos* time, *coram deo* (in God's presence), you will better prioritize the demands placed upon you. Your writing will be more targeted. Your work more energetic.

THE ILLUSION OF "NOT ENOUGH TIME"

I'm afraid I have yet to learn this lesson I read so many years ago: "Avoid the fuss and flurry of the man who is pressed for time. In the realm of the mind, quietness is better than speed. . . . He who knows the value of time always has enough; not being able to lengthen it, he intensifies its value; and first of all he does nothing to shorten it" (A. G. Sertillanges, *The Intellectual Life*).

I used to tell myself and others that I did not have enough time to write. That wasn't entirely accurate. The time existed, but the fatigue I felt usually came from how I apportioned my time. There was more time to write than I thought. We all have the same amount of time, I just hadn't prioritized writing enough. Now, I find the time and take it.

One author breaks down the week this way: Every single one of us has 168 hours in a week. A forty-hour full-time job leaves you 128 hours. After eight hours set aside for sleep each night, you will have seventy-two remaining hours. If you take twenty hours each week to work on writing, you will have fifty-two hours left to do whatever you want to do—collect stamps, ride ferris wheels, learn Mandarin. People will wonder whether you found a secret elixir to get more than the twenty-four hours allotted to the rest of us.

Some people use time as an excuse for poor planning. They live a hurly-burly life. As I mentioned in the chapter on rest, generative people avoid living frenetically. There are varied speeds to the seasons of life, no doubt, but you must move forward. Always forward, never frenetic. Live urgently, but never manically.

As someone once said, "You can have excuses or you can have results, but you cannot have both." People who practice *kairos* living will recognize the inestimable value of each moment, faithfully finding time to write and faithfully serving those whom God has placed in front of them. That kind of person penetrates reality—this earthy, messy life.

REST IN THE GOD OF TIME

In her waning years, my grandmother used to bemoan time. "I just can't hold on to it," she would say. Her failing memory and the sheer speed with which time travels as one ages unnerved her.

"There's no use holding on to a river," a friend told her. "You might as well jump in the water and swim along."

We so desperately want to control time or get more of it or get it back, but maybe God has called us to jump in and swim along. It is his river. Maybe we would enjoy life more if we recognized that reality. Maybe we would trust him more. Maybe we would rest in him a little more easily.

If he can so intimately and beautifully orchestrate a single day like mine in Oxford, he can surely do more than we suspect with our lives. Believe it. Believe that every moment is God's moment and that the flow of time is his. Believe that each day is another grace-filled opportunity to embrace *kairos* time, to trust the hand of God.

THE GRACIOUS HAND OF GOD

The Bible says that Ezra was a man who lived and labored under the good hand of God. He found favor in the eyes of a king because the hand of the Lord his God was on him (Ezra 7:6). He made the long journey back to Jerusalem because "the good hand of his God [was] upon him" (Ezra 7:9). He led God's people courageously because the hand of the Lord was upon him (Ezra 7:28).

What was true of Ezra is true of you and me. We live and labor under the hand of God. He directs our steps. He gives us ideas. He gives us the right words at the right time. He opens doors and closes doors according to his good will. We function in *kairos* time, perpetually and completely under the gracious hand of God. Rejoice, daughter, for this truth gives life so much meaning!

BENEDICTION

I can appreciate Keats who feared that he might die before he had written everything he wanted to write ("When I Have Fears"). I share his fear, as do you. But the Master Storyteller breathed us into the world and has piloted us thus far. Will he not do so to the end?

Until that day when we finally cross Jordan and enter Emmanuel's land, may you value quantity time over quality time. May you labor and laugh, plan and play, eat and edify within *kairos*. Each moment is pregnant! Each moment is meaningful! Each moment is heading toward a revelation!

THE GIFT OF THE MUNDANE

*"No thing is too small for me to cherish
and paint in gold, as if it were an icon
that could bless us."*
—Rainer Maria Rilke, *Book of Hours: Love Poems to God*

A Pennsylvania farmer decided to forgo farming in favor of the oil business. He sold his farm in the early 1900s for $833 and sought his fortune elsewhere. But the new owner of that farm went out to water his cattle one day and found a plank lying on its side across the brook behind the barn. It seemed that the previous owner had placed it there as a kind of dam to prevent a dreadful muck from slipping into the brook's clean water. The new owner had the sludge tested and subsequently uncovered a reserve of coal oil worth one-hundred million dollars.

Dr. Russell Conwell, the founder of Temple University, shared this story many years ago because he knew that people would rather chase fantasies—some of which might come true—than stay where they are and look for treasure there. No one knows whether the original farm owner discovered his sought-after riches, but for over twenty years, he had been sitting on a fortune. We may be tempted to laugh at that poor man, but aren't we guilty of the same? We grow accustomed to the ordinary aspects of life and fail to see them for what they are: treasures.

To me, the modern mind—including mine—marginalizes the mundane and tends to see the ordinary as so much clutter, so many blockades to happiness and peace. Generative writers at their best, however, recognize that the world, especially the ordinary, is jammed with meaning, filled to bursting with the divine. All the small exchanges that weary us with their repetition, the things that make us "sick and tired" are loaded with the luminous, the hiddenness of God, if only we have eyes to see. Teresa of Ávila is credited with saying, "God walks among the pots and pans," and I've found her simple reminder quite provocative. If we're to imitate Christ, then common life—dirty diapers and all—is necessary for generative living. Many writers want to do great things, but forget that lasting success is usually built by doing ordinary things.

INCARNATIONAL LIVING

Remember to imitate Christ who left his father's side to become one of us, to be born under ignoble circumstances, sweat as a carpenter's son, walk in the dust with common fishermen, grow tired like us, bleed like us, eat like us, get sick like us, and cry like us.

Christ's incarnation is proof that God chooses the simple things of the world to baffle the proud, and God chooses the weak things of the world to conquer the strong. He prefers the overlooked and forgotten as his favorite tools to unravel the vain (1 Cor. 1:27-28). The Incarnation also proves that he values ordinariness. Your soul's richness and your writing's subsequent depth depend upon an intimate knowledge of the mundane and tiresome, the threadbare and famished, the repetitious and the unspectacular. Your generative effectiveness depends upon recognizing their value.

Jean Pierre De Caussade once wrote that "no moment is trivial since each one contains a divine kingdom and heavenly sustenance." Each moment, like a seed, is impregnated with the divine, charged with the grandeur of God, a grandeur that loves to inhabit the homely, the discarded, the weak, and the tedious. So remember the duty of the moment, the duty to light your neighbor's path, to fearlessly enter into the grief and gladness of the hearts around you, and to listen to the prompting of the Spirit in that moment.

MUNDANE VS. TRIVIAL

As much as possible, keep your life from being hijacked by busyness and triviality. Life certainly gets busy and it is brim-full of largely mundane things, but there is a significant difference between embracing a mundane life and allowing trivial things to usurp your attention. Mundane activities (like emptying the dishwasher or brushing one's teeth) are the necessary proofs of a healthy life. Trivial activities (like binge-watching comedy shows, cruising the internet, or solving a Rubik's Cube) are a different matter entirely. We can perform endless mundane activities and still remain tuned to mystery and the sacred. But too much triviality robs us of our ability to listen, to contemplate the holy.

I've heard that if you draw a chalk line around a chicken, it will run mindlessly within that circle until it drops from exhaustion. It's a myth told to city slickers in jest, but the picture of a frantic chicken illustrates my point. Many people live like that chicken. They have lost their ability to be still, to listen, to live purposefully. Because you long to live generatively, you will not be among them. Your life will be shaped by the hidden depth and mysterious riches of ordinariness.

THE LAUREL WREATH OF HONOR

I will not romanticize the mundane, nor inflate the glories of laboring under obscurity. I know that even the great Gerard Manley Hopkins felt like "time's eunuch" who could never beget a child. I've shared his frustration. His life's circumstances and relational conflicts perpetually conspired against creative output. They fostered a deep melancholy in him.

J. R. R. Tolkien felt this dilemma, too, and wrote a short story to help resolve his frustrations with the mundane. The story is titled "Leaf by Niggle." It is a must-read for those who feel frustrated by continuous, ordinary demands. By the end of the story (spoiler alert!), Niggle (the protagonist) learns that it was not his masterwork as a painter that mattered most—not his fulfilled dreams—but his daily self-sacrifice and service to others. His mundane labor in obscurity became the laurel wreath of honor he would likely have missed had he focused solely on his creative ambitions.

THE DUTY OF DAILY DEMANDS

We are Christians, which places upon us certain obligations. We're called to faithfulness in little things—doing the dishes, picking up socks, vacuuming, weeding the garden, grading papers, answering emails, changing the oil in the car—treating each moment as a sacrifice to the Lord. We're duty-bound. Duty is not a dirty, four-letter word, it is an opportunity for virtue to shine. It is the demonstration of love well-ordered despite undesirable circumstances. Those unmagical chores are not ancillary to a writer's generative calling and vocation, they are essential. They keep us grounded.

People who surround themselves with real life—the patter of little feet and the home repair—are rarely sentimental or egocentric. Unbeknownst to us, God uses the mundane tasks and mundane hours to enliven life. They become the seedbed for our ideas. Writing instincts erode without them. Take you and your siblings for example. You have given me hundreds of anecdotes and asked thousands of questions. You know all my foibles. You know my failures as a father. You know how to tease me and thereby keep me down-to-earth. I have a difficult time, thankfully, sneaking off to an ivory tower with all this ordinariness swirling around me.

THE GIFT OF AN ORDINARY LIFE AND A FULL-TIME JOB

One of those ordinary things in life is a full-time job. To you, a full-time job might sound like the penultimate roadblock to your hopes, the doorway into a dreary adulthood, the final death knell of your happy childhood.

I remember the feeling. But this mountain journey of faith is a long one and a full-time job is required for most of us to pay the bills. A few all-stars jump into fame and glory right out of the gate. Others suddenly inherit a windfall. I would not wish such a dramatic change in status on my worst enemies. The human heart tends to collapse beneath the pressures of sudden wealth and the resulting implosion is catastrophic. If you were one of those unfortunate few, I would have no advice, having never tasted anything like it. Since you are, thankfully, like the rest of us and must plan to hold down a day job, here are some helpful reminders.

First, the very notion of a "day job" has demeaning connotations. It sounds like something less important than what you would rather be doing like, say, writing. You cannot afford to think this way. If you do, your day job will suffer. Saving your energy for your writing, you will do poor work elsewhere. This is a bad testimony of your God and a blight on your character. Furthermore, there are many jobs—especially those that include people—that are impossible to do well if your heart is elsewhere. Effective teaching, as one example, cannot be accomplished half-heartedly. Learn to put your full energies—heart, soul, mind, and body—into your day job and your writing. It is possible. Neither should suffer for lack of your best effort.

Second, a day job is not a "necessary evil." God has called us to work. He has made us to work. Despite popular misconception, we will work in the New Creation. Some people—artists included—bifurcate "real work" from creative endeavors, but no such distinction exists for Christians. Everything we do, everything to which we put our minds and hands, we do in the name of God and for the sake of his kingdom. Some jobs are certainly more tedious than others and some seem to meet a cultural need more obviously than others, but any jobs that are not forbidden by God are worth valuing and doing well.

Third, a day job offers plenty of valuable experience and opportunity for writers. Live like a wine collector who, every single day, collects some vintage and stores it in the cellar of his heart and mind where it ripens until ready to be enjoyed, richer, deeper, and more loved for its many years in waiting. Store those choice vintages—the words, the relationships, the victories, the defeats—in the cellar of your heart and mind.

Fourth, a day job offers new relationships, new self-discoveries, new opportunities to expand a skill set. As a result, a day job tethers the heart to certain places and people. When old, you will remember some of them fondly. A day job also forces you into uncomfortable situations that may reveal something new about you or about others. Those revelations are helpful for you and they will inform your writing. While the work you do may not be as thrilling to you as writing, it equips you to serve people in unexpected ways down the road.

These are all gifts from God. Do not avoid them, embrace them, and remember that at the end of the day, your job—no matter what you're doing—is to follow God. Jesus's first and last words to Peter were "Follow me." Those are his first and last words to you, too.

BENEDICTION

May you embrace your duties heartily, one day at a time. May you marinate in the places and people of your life. May you submerge yourself completely in ordinariness for the sake of your God, for the sake of your people, and for the sake of your writing.

COMMUNITY AND SOLITUDE

"The first stars hover and drift down. Like a roosting hawk, I listen to the silence and gaze into the dark."
—J. A. Baker, *The Peregrine*

Out of five-hundred plus in my graduating class, I was voted most likely to become a monk. No, I didn't find it funny at the time, but after nearly twenty-five years of marriage and five children, I can laugh about it now. Mine isn't exactly the monastic life, but I know why they voted that way. I've always been at ease with solitude. I was the kid who would rather be left alone most of the time, free to think his own thoughts and do his own thing, a textbook introvert. Even today I feel most at home in solitude, and most like a foreigner in crowds.

Maybe that's why this quotation from Bonhoeffer's *Life Together* keeps nagging at me. You read it to me yesterday because you share my aversion to crowds. I'm glad you gave it to me. His words have prompted me to meditate on the paradox of community, the necessity of being alone and together.

"Let him who cannot be alone beware of community. He will only do harm to himself and to the community. Alone you stood before God when he called you; alone you had to answer that call; alone you had to struggle and pray; and alone you will die and give an account to God ...

But the reverse is also true: Let him who is not in community beware of being alone. Into the community you were called, the call was not meant for you alone."

CALLED TO SERVE COMMUNITY

God calls you to serve community. Your community is more than your family and friends. It includes coworkers and strangers, too. Generative Christians engender loyalty and trust and affection from those people. We build relationships, not simply platforms. The former tend to stay people-centered, while the latter are focused on income and influence. Neither hardship nor prosperity should derail the proper prioritization of people over prestige. Christ prioritized people over power in this way and you're an extension of his love.

GENERATIVITY THRIVES IN COMMUNITY

I've been surprised in life to find that my writing generates in those around me new creative expressions that, in turn, inspire me to further work. This picture coincides with the garden metaphor. When I cultivate the garden around me—weeding, watering, planting, and fertilizing—those plants blossom and send forth their own shoots, their own seeds on the wind. You will find this principle true in your own life.

Join a community that shares your love for God, for people, and for life. Share poetry together. Send each other quotations from the books you're reading. Encourage them in their endeavors. That community is an important part of sustaining you on life's journey. Eat together, play together, work together, and forgive each other.

All communities are prone to flattery, passivity, gossip, alliances, or jealousy. That is no reason to avoid groups. Patiently work through those things together, candidly honoring each other and helping each other to greater faithfulness. If you learn to depend upon others, your community will guard you from lusts of the mind, from pride, and from an inordinate self-reliance. Fear these things as much as you fear the lusts of the flesh. They are equally dangerous to the soul.

THE POWER OF COMMUNITY

For good or ill, people living in community share with each other, compounding their resulting growth. This isn't always a good thing. The flu, for example, spreads rapidly, building momentum within a community as its victims increase in number. Gossip has a similar contagious quality—be it in a family or a class at school, and technology and social networks only accelerate the speed and extend the reach. That's the bad news.

The good news is that many positive things are contagious, too, such as laughter or a strong work ethic. Gladness and hope are also contagious. Generativity is contagious. Friends who labor together for the same cause impact culture more effectively than one person who works in isolation.

We desperately need community. Isolation amplifies our vulnerability and multiplies our insufficiencies. The human heart's downward drag will inevitably shift our vision from Christ to self, from faith to fear, from dependance to self-reliance. We need other people to remind us of God's faithfulness and conquering work. We need them to keep us from trusting in our own strength. And we need others to lift our eyes to Jesus as we help them lift theirs. We have a responsibility to cultivate an upward orientation in the community God has given to us.

Consequently, one of the most important decisions we have to make is whom to befriend. Proverbs 13:20 says, "He who walks with wise men will be wise, but the companion of fools will be destroyed." So find people whose faith seems stronger than yours, whose eyes are more fixed on the Lord than yours, and who verbalize thanks more often than you. Watch them. Imitate them. Walk with them. Eat meals with them. Pray for them. Thank them. Be vulnerable with them without dragging them down into your own self-pity. Fight the urge to become a vortex of selfishness.

Finally, the great power of community rests on its ability to engender thankfulness. Where people serve each other, pray for each other, weep with each other, and laugh with each other, thankfulness abounds. Thanksgiving, like praise, gives the heart an outward orientation. Maybe God calls us to community in part because being alone for too long turns our attention onto ourselves. The more we verbalize thankfulness, the more we forget about ourselves. We start noticing others and what they are doing. We start finding reasons to be thankful. Ultimately, we start seeing abundance instead of scarcity. Start asking yourself, "How can I thank the person right in front me?" A teacher, mother, sister, stranger? Learn to ask, "What is God giving me right now?"

Ultimately, your work is largely meaningless apart from community. You need readers, right? You need editors, right? You need to bounce your ideas off of others, right? Your writing is formed by others and for others. This realization should not surprise us since God is three persons in one, a community. He made us in his image and designed us for relationship. For this reason, the two greatest commandments offered by Christ to summarize the law given to Moses were to "love the Lord your God with all your heart, mind, and strength," and to "love your neighbor as yourself." Love, as found in God and described in his word, requires community.

WRITING IS LONELY WORK

Yes, we're called into life together, but I couldn't be a writer without time alone. Writing usually happens in solitude. Most of the time, I have to generate ideas alone, too. I certainly have to agonize alone. More often than not, I must motivate myself to work and keep myself determined as well. Other people stay involved, encouraging where they can, but actually running the engine, maintaining the engine, and driving the engine somewhere are my job and mine alone.

I think you will find this true in your own life. The real substantive work must happen in your own heart and mind. You still have to wake up on your own and start writing. Once you are out of school, no one will make you do it. I doubt this news discourages you because you're already wired to carry the writer's lonely burden. But you may find that the hardest thing to do is find time alone. Something always intrudes.

SOLITUDE VS. ISOLATION

I do not refer to family or friends who have every right to intrude, I refer to the myriad technologies that beckon to us: smartphones, social networks, immediate news alerts, YouTube. Despite our best efforts, we simply do not have the godlike ability to absorb and attend to so much information. As a result, I think our spiritual depths have shallowed, our inner landscapes have shrunk. Information's incessant assault has made solitude—mental quietude—nearly impossible.

Ironically, with this decrease of solitude has come an increase of isolation. The differences are subtle but important. Both words describe time alone. Solitude is sought by those who want mental space to think and fill the heart's tank before returning to community. Isolation, however, is sought by those who want to be alone and who will put up any wall to stay there. Solitude does not push others away like isolation does. Or look at this way: love desires solitude; selfishness desires isolation. Christ desired solitude; an angry teenager wants isolation.

Isolation amplifies the ego's siren song; solitude exposes the heart's unbridled babble. Solitude also affords the opportunity to feel mystery and immensity while encouraging an awareness of the inner life that relentless busyness and fear tend to arrest. In solitude, silence asserts itself.

For these and many other reasons, isolation is qualitatively different from solitude. God blesses a measured amount of the latter; the former is a sign of the curse: "A man who isolates himself seeks his own desire; he rages against all wise judgment" (Prov. 18:1). God did not make you to be alone in a permanent sense. Such aloneness goes against his Trinitarian nature.

Those who stay isolated for too long end up lonely. But that's the world in which we live. Despite our increased connectivity, our homes have become isolation cells where we eat alone, watch TV alone, and sleep alone. Even within families, we push each other away. In private or public, we plug in to escape.

I write these paragraphs while sitting in a shopping mall's lounge. I'm taking advantage of the moment while I wait for friends. Five candy and soda dispensers line the wall to my left. From two enormous televisions on the wall, sports commentators analyze an athlete's ten-second failure. They are animated, but I cannot hear them over the clambering children, the exasperated adults, and the pop music pumping over the speakers. I've plugged in my earbuds to drown out the banging noises with noises of my own choosing. The irony of my situation is not lost on me.

So I'm faced with this reality and my own failure to handle it well. Can I concentrate only by plugging in my earbuds? Is solitude only possible with virtual detachment from reality? And when I detach in this way, do I usher in a loneliness I did not expect?

LEARNING TO VALUE SOLITUDE

Our Lord Jesus used solitude as a means of preparing for community and for work. If Christ needed to be alone in a boat or alone amongst the hills when he wanted to fellowship with his father, who are we to think that our souls will thrive on a diet of distraction and perpetual productivity? We need to get away, but we rarely do, so the pre-Socratic philosopher, Meno, asks a question still pertinent today: "How will you go about finding that thing the nature of which is totally unknown to you?" If solitude and mental quietude are utterly foreign to us, how are we supposed to experience them? How are we supposed to recognize them when we see them? I pause and stare out the window. I have no answer. Or maybe this moment *is* an answer.

I have so much to learn. I'm trying to live out the paradox of community, taking time to be alone and living faithfully in community. I try to find small moments of solitude, no matter my station or duties in life. I try not to lie to myself about how little time I actually need to get away. I need less time for solitude than I generally think, but more than the world will offer. I've found that more-frequent though shorter times of solitude are better than infrequent but long ones. A short walk is often enough.

Dorothy Sayers remarked that while our lives are flooded with words, we do not know what the words mean, nor how to fight them or fling them back. She says we're prey to propaganda, but believe ourselves masters of our desires and convictions. If she is right, then humanity is currently in a pitiful position. I think part of the reason for our societal gullibility is the lack of solitude. We have no quiet spaces in which the mind can think carefully, the heart can long for transcendent things, and the soul can stretch toward God. Contemplation is an endangered practice.

BENEDICTION

May you learn to be alone and together. May you always love community, but may you also love solitude. Truly, "solitude is the homeland of the strong, silence is their prayer" (Gustave Delacroix de Ravignan).

ANXIETY

"Worrying doesn't empty tomorrow of its sorrow, it empties today of its strength."

—Corrie ten Boom

Your grandfather served as the only doctor to a small hospital in Kenya for nearly six years while I played "football" with my friends using a soccer ball made of plastic bags tied tightly together with twine. I often wandered the countryside gnawing on sugar cane. I learned early to always watch the branches above me for green mambas, deadly snakes that like to fall on their prey from above. And I learned to watch the path in front of me for spitting cobras, to turn my face away quickly and run because their venom blinds. It was not a fear-filled childhood, but I stayed alert.

One day, the old man who lived across the way ran out of his house and started beating the tall grasses with his thick staff. Dad joined him with a shovel while I watched. In short order, they dragged a mangled, eight-foot cobra toward our front steps. I climbed out of the avocado tree and followed my dad. He stretched it out on the porch and marveled at it for some time. Then he announced his brilliant plan.

"Son! Let's hang this thing over your shoulders and get a picture of you flexing like Tarzan!" It was a great idea in theory. I don't blame dad for what happened next.

I hardly ever wore a shirt in that tropical weather, so I posed bare-chested while my dad draped the snake over my shoulders. I gripped its tail with my left hand and its head with my right. He walked several paces away and was fiddling with the camera when I felt the snake move over my neck—just a little. Then I felt the snake's body push through my hands. Paralyzed, I could not speak. A silent scream contorted my face.

Dad looked up, saw my terror, and said, "Don't worry, son, the snake's dead. But it still has electricity moving through its body. It's just a reflexive movement." As if that fixed anything! I hurled the cobra away and saw it mechanically coil on the ground as I ran for the house.

From that day forward, snakes have terrified me. Even as a grown man, I can't walk through a pet store without shying away from the glass reptile tanks and breaking into a cold sweat.

When you were about three years old, we took a family trip to Colorado in the summer. Our little car had poor air conditioning and the day was hot, so we pulled over for a picnic at an enormous park, probably five acres in size. We found a shaded area and unpacked our food.

I munched on my sandwich contemplatively, watching an old truck pull up at the far end of the park. The driver climbed out and pulled down his tailgate. To my astonishment, a gigantic python thumped heavily to the ground and slithered through the grass.

Panic heaved in my heart and my throat constricted. I couldn't even swallow, though the snake was still a good two hundred feet away or more. Then it stopped moving and lifted its head as if scanning the park for something. Its eyes pointed our direction and froze for just a moment. Then it lowered its head and rushed toward us. Maybe it smelled our food, I don't know, but I wasn't sticking around to find out. I grabbed the keys, snatched you up in the car seat, and ran for the car. "You can come or you can stay, but we're leaving now!" I yelled. Your poor mother.

"Why?" she asked.

"Snake," was all I could say.

She bundled up the picnic blanket and remaining food, threw them into the trunk, and leapt into the car. She barely had the door shut before I peeled out of the parking lot.

She knew my story. I had warned her. She knew that snakes scared me, but she had never seen my flight or fight response in action.

FACING REALITY

I've heard that we're born with only two fears: the fear of falling and the fear of loud noises. If true, this reinforces the very real fact that we accumulate fears over time. We undoubtedly manufacture some, but life-experiences saddle us with the others. From worry to severe anxiety disorders, from run-of-the-mill fears to irrational phobias, all writers live somewhere on anxiety's broad spectrum. Whether fear of snakes or fear of failure, fear is a universal human dilemma. We fear heights, spiders, bats, public speaking, rejection letters, financial collapse, negative reviews, loneliness, memory loss—the list is endless. And these fears bang incessantly on the tin-roofing of our fragile hearts.

And if anxiety were not paralyzing enough, it brings discouragement along for company. We feel unique. We feel alone. We wallow in our weakness. We listen to fear's lies, fully knowing that they are lies. We look in the mirror each morning and wonder when fear will finally stop being an unwanted house guest. And just when we think anxiety has finally packed its bags, we see a deadline looming or a speaking engagement approaching with terrifying inevitability. Anxiety rises. We lose heart. Even those of us who know and trust Christ struggle with anxiety.

History offers a long list of faithful God-followers who fought anxiety or depression, some for much of their lives. Moses, Gideon, Jeremiah, Job, Elijah, Jonah, Hannah, even King David struggled—as evidenced by his psalms—though he had tasted remarkable courage many times, even defeating a lion, a bear, and Goliath. Charles Spurgeon, William Cowper, G. K. Chesterton, and Mother Teresa likewise struggled. Some suffocated so badly beneath the weight that they entertained suicidal thoughts not once, but many times.

Anxiety does not discriminate. It takes the strong and the weak, the cheerful and the melancholy, the spiritual juggernaut and the spiritual lightweight. It will take us sick or healthy, rich or poor, sinner or saint. Athletes, chefs, doctors, therapists, nutritionists, teachers, mothers, fathers, and priests are not immune.

Anxiety is an enormous problem facing God's people, and writers wrestle with more than their fair share. Addressing the topic is complicated by ambiguity. The line between anxiety and worry, for example, is not as clear as we would like. What is chemically induced and what is not? When is the brain working improperly and when are we simply fretting. When is panic a biological reflex and when is it self induced?

I cannot offer easy answers, nor easy solutions. Anxiety is real. Anxiety is powerful and, in some cases, even deadly. We dare not treat it lightly. Those who have fallen down the rabbit hole of depression know the seriousness of anxiety. They also have learned the hard way that the world is uncomfortably silent or unhelpfully trite on the subject. Even Christians squirm around the topic. Some people are downright flippant in their judgments, shaming vulnerable people into silence rather than serving them.

In a classic Bob Newhart skit, a young woman seeks counsel for her claustrophobia. She is terribly afraid of being buried alive in a box. He says that his psychotherapy sessions last only five minutes and they come with two important words which she is to incorporate into her life: "Stop it!" That's it. To Newhart's character, recovery is as simple as that.

Those who have never stood on the edge of a mental breakdown and those who have never suffocated beneath depression's heavy hand find the skit funnier than those who have. If "Stop it!" were all we needed to conquer the giant, Anxiety, then it would not have so many carcass trophies hanging on its wall.

We've tried "stopping it." It's harder than it sounds. We would like to sleep peacefully at night. We would like to wake up eager for the day. We would like to be courageous and hopeful and glad. Instead, the giant keeps entering our valley, wreaking havoc on our happiness. And for some strange reason, we still think that anxiety can only be defeated by sheer willpower. Our mortal vantage point is woefully insufficient for helping us deal with our repeated failure to defeat it.

STANDING ON THE PROMISES

God's promises provide a new vantage point, a divine perspective that we all need, especially writers:

He says, "Fear not, for I am with you; Be not dismayed, for I am your God. I will strengthen you, Yes, I will help you, I will uphold you with my righteous right hand" (Isa. 41:10).

And he says, "For I know the thoughts that I think toward you . . . thoughts of peace and not of evil, to give you a future and a hope" (Jer. 29:11).

1 Peter 5:7 says we can cast the whole weight of our anxieties upon God because we're his personal concern. Romans 8:28 confirms that promise: "And we know that all things work

together for good to those who love God, to those who are called according to his purpose."

These are not Pollyanna promises. Nor are they mere talismans against dark forces. In a seismic spiritual earthquake, they are the firm, unshakable ground on which we stand. God has not promised many things in life, but he has promised that we have no cause to fear—even when giants attack—because he is at work.

Belief in these promises changes how God's children hear the everyday question, "How are you doing?" If God is faithful to keep his promises, then in an ultimate sense, we can truthfully answer, "Everything is going my way." He intimately uses my circumstances, even the scary ones, for my benefit. All the time. Guaranteed.

Anyone who answers that way risks sounding pompous, or at the very least presumptuous. But what if we answered that way in our minds? Would we start seeing differently? Would we see opportunity where others see limitation? Would we see abundance where others see scarcity? Would our thankfulness, gladness, and peace grow? No matter the circumstance? Perhaps.

THE GOOD NEWS

"Anxiety in the heart of man causes depression, but a good word makes it glad," says Proverbs 12:25. Here's a good word:

Instead of demanding that you toughen up, God asks you to look up. Look to the One who has already entered the valley to fight on your behalf. God didn't give us the story of David and Goliath so that we could live more courageously and take down Anxiety. He gave us the story so that in every daunting circumstance, we would see Jesus. If we had to fight anxiety by our own willpower, then all hope would be lost.

What David said to Saul, Jesus says to us regarding fear: "Let no man's heart fail because of him [Goliath]; your servant will go and fight. . . . Your servant has killed both lion and bear; and this uncircumcised Philistine will be like one of them, seeing he has defied the armies of the living God" (1 Sam. 17:32, 36).

Even David knew that he was not the conquering hero of the story: "The Lord, who delivered me from the paw of the lion and from the paw of the bear, he will deliver me from the hand of this Philistine" (1 Sam. 17:37). Not me, but God! And Paul echoes this conviction when he says, "It is no longer I who live, but Christ lives in me; and the life which I now live in the flesh I live by faith in the Son of God, who loved me and gave Himself for me" (Gal. 2:20).

Not me, but God!

AN INVERTED GOSPEL

If we're honest, the Gospel message has been diluted by the American Dream and now sounds something like this in our minds: "Christ died for you so that you could do all things." But that's not the Gospel. The Gospel message is this: Jesus is the fulfillment of God's promises—every last one of them—and he smote all of God's enemies and won back God's children. When he died on the cross, he said, "It is finished!" Done. Past tense. Permanently. When Paul writes, "I can do all things through Christ who strengthens me" (Phil. 4:13), he is pointing at Christ who does the work, not himself.

Worry reigns when we try to fix that which only God can fix, or handle what only he can handle, or know what only he can know. Worry says, "This situation is entirely up to me," when it is actually up to God. The solution to fear is not courage, it is faith. Who gives us faith but God? We cannot drum it up by our own willpower. It is a gift. Dare we ask for more faith? That is a prayer that God delights to answer, but many of us are too busy worrying to ask for it.

THE POWER OF MEMORIZED SCRIPTURE

What do we do when myriad taunts wake us in the morning and dog us during the day? We inevitably talk about what captures our gaze. Those who worry about illness talk perpetually about illness. Those who fear economic collapse talk about the country's financial volatility. We worry about the kids, about Uncle Drew's smoking habit, about Grandma's heart disease and these things fill our conversations (if not our conversations with others, then certainly those internally).

That is why God tells us to fill our mouths with his praise and to meditate on his word day and night (Ps. 1:2). That is why God calls us to lift our eyes, look to Jesus, see what God sees, and speak it. These activities lift our vision from the snakes at our feet to the King who came and conquered. I've found this particular psalm helpful in shifting my view:

Psalm 16:8-11:
I have set the Lord always before me;
Because He is at my right hand I shall not be moved.
Therefore my heart is glad, and my glory rejoices;
My flesh also will rest in hope.
For you will not leave my soul in Sheol,
Nor will you allow your Holy One to see corruption.
You will show me the path of life;
In your presence is fullness of joy;
At your right hand are pleasures forevermore.

This passage changes my mental soundtrack and reorients my imagination. It points out reality and gives my heart an upward orientation. It's actually difficult to stay anxious while my mouth repeatedly declares, *I have set the Lord always before me; Because He is at my right hand I shall not be moved. Therefore my heart is glad, and my glory rejoices!*

WE ARE BLESSED

The most compelling reason not to fear is that God loves to bless. He has blessed us in the past. He is blessing us now. And he will bless in the future. The world overflows with gratuitous gifting. It is impossible to list all of the good things God has made in the world for our benefit. The very fact that God makes the rain to fall on the just and unjust is proof that God loves to bless.

Wherever and whenever we find anxiety climbing, God still gives us his blessing. For God's children, life's varied moments are opportunities to remember God's presence and his provision. Your Lord—the one who rose and lives again—is the one who said, "Come to me, all you who labor and are heavy laden, and I will give you rest" (Matt. 11:28). He is, indeed, a refuge and a fortress, the one in whom we trust (Ps. 91:2).

Is your heart heavy laden? You're not alone. Say to yourself, "I will call upon the Lord, who is worthy to be praised; so shall I be saved from my enemies" (Ps. 18:3). All you need to do is wake up, look up, and call upon his name. Is that so difficult to do?

A FINAL CAUTION

It occurs to me as I write this letter, that I've never talked to my dad about his experience with that cobra so many years ago. I've never asked him about his side of the story. I've never asked him if he was afraid. I've never asked him if he was almost bitten when he killed it with his shovel. I've never asked him if he had other close calls with deadly snakes during those years in Kenya. And so here is one often-overlooked result of anxiety. It makes us think about ourselves too much. We forget others. We forget God.

BENEDICTION

May you remember that you cannot defeat anxiety on your own. You were never meant to do so, dear daughter. God has already sent Jesus into your valley to defeat it. Practice daily gratitude for his presence and his provision.

SUFFERING

"Everything happens as if poets had a special mission, as if they had to give an example that only they can give, as if their life, whatever it may be, was willed to be as it is."
—François Mauriac, *Second Thoughts*

I met surprise at sixty miles-per-hour on a freeway I drive quite regularly. I had the road nearly to myself one night. The rain was beating down, but my windshield wipers worked perfectly fine. My little Toyota's headlights probed the darkness. Nothing seemed out of the ordinary, until my headlights illuminated something large and heavy—like a concrete construction divider—directly in front of me. With no time to hit the brakes, I swerved, only clipping the object with my fender.

I pulled the car over, trying hard to breathe slowly while my heart felt like it might jump out of my chest. Had I drifted off to sleep? Had I entered a construction zone? What was it? The unlit freeway gave no clues. I backed the car along the shoulder until I could see better. To my shock, I saw that the object was an eight-foot couch.

Perplexed, I climbed out of the car and stood in the rain. Did it fall off of a truck? What kind of moron loses a couch off the back of his truck? But then I noticed that it was upright, set exactly in the middle of the three lanes at the darkest point of the road. It didn't tumble off of a truck, it was set there. On purpose. Some bored kids probably wanted to see someone get lit up like a Christmas tree. And I almost did.

I dragged it off of the road and climbed into my car, shaken. Questions stormed my mind. What if I had glanced away for a split second? What if I hadn't swerved? You'll laugh, but the entire drive home, I kept waiting for another couch to appear. I have no idea who left that couch there, but even to this day I stay alert for couches when I drive freeways at night—especially on rainy nights. Strange, I know. But that's how it is. Close encounters with death change one's perspective. Suddenly, I was different.

And that is how suffering feels to us: like a sudden obstruction in our way. Like a divine couch dropped in the road—and if not dodged it may wreck us. Some people seem to rarely suffer. Others spend all of their efforts trying to dodge it. Still others seem condemned to run into suffering repeatedly at full speed.

SUFFERING, OUR COMMON LOT

We're all in the hands of God, and while that is always a good and promising thing, the Scriptures do not shy away from the universal reality of human suffering: ". . . man is born to trouble, as the sparks fly upward" (Job 5:7). Even God enfleshed, our Lord Jesus, suffered in every way we do—physically, mentally, emotionally, spiritually, relationally. I treasure Matthew 26 as a personal comfort because it describes Jesus staggering beneath the weight of suffering: "My soul is exceedingly sorrowful, even to death" (v. 38). Recognizing that cry for what it is helps remove the common, though unnecessary, stigma attached to suffering and sorrow. They are part of the human condition, especially when the soul is under duress.

Truly, suffering is more poignant at some times than at others, but it is the undercurrent of existence, nonetheless. When suffering is greatest, when we stagger in a desert, sometimes we find God waiting there, drawing us out to meet him. I described my own encounter with suffering in *A Small Cup of Light*, although it was difficult to re-enter my pain, to write about it. The book gave me the opportunity to be utterly vulnerable regarding the alienation and spiritual struggle that suffering prompts, but it also testifies to the faithfulness of God no matter the circumstances.

I know that suffering has impacted me in at least one important way—it has forced my reliance upon God. Sickness, grief, loss, loneliness, bewilderment, and alienation have all forced me into a vulnerability I did not like, but left me grasping for God. This dependency is a good thing, dear child. It is, in fact, a significant goal of the Christian journey. Alistair Begg is correct, weakness is advantageous when dependency is the goal. We were not designed for autonomy, to be masters of our own fates. We were made for relationship with God who knows our mortality. That is why we need not fear suffering.

SUFFERING SHAPES US FOR MEANINGFUL EXPRESSION

Believe it or not, suffering and creativity are not enemies. Life's troubles are often the seedbed of deeply meaningful writing and creative acts, especially for artists who perpetually use their life experiences to serve others. Suffering prepares us to sing exquisite songs, to spangle the darkness with bright stars.

Yes, suffering makes us feel naked. Yes, suffering reminds us of our weakness. We grieve. But it seems to me that the writer's job is to wait upon the Lord who hides his face and to look for him the world over (Isa. 8:17)—to stay awake in suffering and out of suffering, to find evidence of him in every circumstance for the sake of deeper creativity, no matter the sorrow, no matter the strife.

The best writers take every opportunity to explore the complexity, ambiguity, and paradox of life—all of it—to record upon their cave walls the illumination of a life. This is precisely the generational, inspirational, and generous work to which we're called. Our vulnerability reveals beauty hidden within and beyond.

I think we would be surprised by the poignant misery that served as inspiration for some of the most celebrated works of human expression. How many artists have suffered from isolation, poverty, deformity, or social exile? Milton wrote despite blindness. Bach, van Gogh, and Dickens composed while suffering what was likely bipolar disorder. Keats died young from pulmonary tuberculosis. Blake and Wilde died penniless. Byron's club foot, Stevenson's frailty, and Emily Dickinson's struggle with isolation and mental illness are well-documented. History is proof that suffering and creativity are not enemies.

Readers intuitively perceive that darkness has deepened and strengthened these authors' works. We're moved because they recorded their yearnings and their yearnings are ours. This creativity born from suffering reinforces a principle that God wove into the fabric of creation, namely, that a grain of wheat must fall into the ground and die before it bears fruit (John 12:24). Why do readers feel a magnetic pull toward generative writers? Because they sense a shared experience, an empathy and depth of insight that simultaneously comforts and enriches them.

François Mauriac believed that God does not treat poets as he does the rest of humanity. He noted that for poets, everything happens as if it were tailor-made for them, and they are to give an account, a testimony that they alone can give, as if their lives were specially built to say what they are meant to say. I think he's correct. Poets have tailor-made experiences that equip them for a particular kind of writing.

Your life experience is creativity's soil, but other people's suffering can also provide grounding for your writing. Their loss, grief, and pain may generate profound thoughts in you—visions of the divine that you were meant to share with the world. You don't have to experience all of humanity's trouble first-hand to be an effective writer. All you need is empathy. Your generative effectiveness will be closely tied to your ability to empathize with those around you who have hit rock bottom.

I heard it said by one who has greater faith than I, that rock bottom is solid ground for the Christian. She was right. God is the rock upon which you will fall, but even there upon that rock you can sit in the dark . . . and dream. Allow your life experiences, good and bad, to be the crucible of your ideas, conversations, and work. Allow your life to bloom beneath the pressures of your situation, whatever it is.

ENGAGEMENT, NOT AVOIDANCE

I fear for writers whose hearts feed strictly on the superficial happiness of a comfortable and positive life by fleeing "negative" emotions. They will fall victim to the misconception that God wants merely conformity and obedience, forgetting that God wants our full engagement with him. In so doing, they will confuse joy with happiness, grief with abject despair. They will start writing sentimental kitsch.

If the Psalms are a songbook for God's people, then we should find insight and encouragement in the fact that it does not include 150 happy songs. What we find in the Psalms are honest encounters with grief and gladness, loss and life, bewilderment and boldness, rage and rejoicing. Each song was written in light of the conviction that God is good, faithful, and in charge. They each point the quailing human heart to the rock of salvation and remind us of our rightful place in the hands of God.

Thomas à Kempis penned this beautiful prayer that echoes the message of the Psalms: "If you wish me to be in darkness, I shall bless you. And if you wish me to be in light, again I shall bless you. If you stoop down to comfort me, I shall bless you, and if you wish me to be afflicted, I shall bless you forever" (*The Imitation of Christ*). Far from being disheartening, these psalm-like prayers embolden us to trust our Maker and Sustainer in the midst of suffering.

They remind us not to hurry nor bustle our way through to the other side of suffering, but to sit in the darkness and wait on God. There in the darkness, I know that God is present and active, doing something transformative in us, not because suffering is specially made to transform us but because God is always in the process of transformation.

I encourage you to stay committed to living thankfully in the moment, whether sorrow-filled or full of happiness. Yes, life is risky. Whatever you do to guard against risk will prevent you from experiencing joy in its fullness. You may not want the suffering, but by being open to risk, you open yourself to joy.

THE TEMPTATION TO COMPLAIN

Above all else, I would ask you not to engage in a pattern of complaint. You have made certain decisions about your life now as a generative writer and must learn to face the frustrations. Loneliness, loss, and human weakness will likely be some of them. Stay focused and resolute throughout. Write. You will meet with grief, bewilderment, failures of many kinds, but if you abandon yourself freely to this calling, then these small deaths will no longer loom so large. You will learn from them and move on to a second birth and a third birth, reborn after each death.

What God takes away, when he takes it away, will be its own kind of death. Nevertheless, in God we find life. Our deaths are nothing but divine opportunities to discover God's life-giving nature. As I've learned through my own health issues, those seasons when my mental faculties suffered have not changed his goodness. When I thought my life was crumbling down around me, he was opening my narrow life onto more hope, more beauty, more life.

Consider it a possibility, even if a remote one, that God knows how your suffering will be the very thing that propels you to better generative service. When you feel far from God, unable to see the world charged with his grandeur, do not panic, just latch onto those who do see it. Read them, talk to them, listen to them, watch them, walk with them, and ride their coat-tails. But give your fear to God.

You will forever be dogged by your changeableness because we live in a broken world. You will swing between hilarity and deep sadness, anxiety and absolute peace, faithfulness and unfaithfulness, sincerity and flippancy. But God is unchanging and the one to whom, through all your changing, you should direct the ear of your heart, awake to his voice. He is immutable, unchanging, the ground of being.

GOD RENEWS YOUR STRENGTH

On my way home from work one evening, I began to experience strong tremors through my torso and arms. The muscles in my face began to lilt and my cognition slowed to a crawl. All signs pointed to a stroke, but I knew I was not having a stroke. My heart rate was normal and, when we later checked it, so was my blood pressure. By the time I arrived home, my hands had turned in on themselves, growing rigid like someone who suffers from cerebral palsy. Although I was unstressed, my nervous system was malfunctioning in frightening ways. My children, somewhat accustomed to my health condition by then, still found my appearance alarming. They helped me to a chair where I could safely sit and wait for the symptoms to subside.

I asked my son to bring me my Bible because I needed something to distract me from my pain and worries. He did so and with my rigid hands, I cracked the covers and let it fall open. The first verse I read was Psalm 144:1 which says, "Blessed be the Lord my rock, who trains my hands for war, and my fingers for battle."

I laughed out loud. Ironies abounded. I had every reason to dismiss this verse, to find in it no application for my life. But I was struck by the stunning coincidence and I was forced to ask, "What if I did not turn to this verse on accident? What if I was meant to read it? What if this verse holds true for me even now in my present condition?"

I have no tightly organized argument to explain how that verse was true for me in that moment, but I know it was true nonetheless—if not literally, then in some other way. I have faith that it was true. It reminded me of another passage written for those who suffer in the world and wonder whether God is paying any attention at all.

Isaiah 40:27-31:
"Why do you say, O Jacob,
And speak, O Israel: 'My way is hidden from the Lord, and my just claim is passed over by my God'? Have you not known? Have you not heard? The everlasting God, the Lord, the creator of the ends of the earth, neither faints nor is weary. His understanding is unsearchable. He gives power to the weak, and to those who have no might he increases strength. Even the youths shall faint and be weary, and the young men shall utterly fall, but those who wait on the Lord shall renew their strength; they shall mount up with wings like eagles, they shall run and not be weary, they shall walk and not faint."

We believe God's promises to be true. We believe that his understanding surpasses our own. We believe that he gives power to the weak. But sometimes these things are hard to see, difficult to believe. Even still, God renews our strength when we wait on him in our suffering.

In a mysterious way, he is mounting us up on eagles' wings. In a way perhaps we do not understand, he is helping us to run and not grow weary, to walk and not faint. None of this is possible apart from a God who works mysteriously and paradoxically. None of this will be realized apart from faithfully trusting him and taking his hand.

WALK INTO THE DARKNESS, HAND IN HAND WITH GOD

The sun is setting behind the towering pines of your childhood. Let your soul shine radiantly, pulsing with spiritual life and charged with purpose. You already stand upon that immovable ground of being whether you feel it or not. Today I awoke with my memory alive, filled by vivid snapshots of your childhood. Ponytails, freckles, long fingers pressed to my face, reading books beneath your bed by flashlight in hopes that I would not come downstairs and find you awake past your bedtime.

I remember reading the promises of God and asking him to keep them in your life. There were days that my faith faltered, but God steadily carried you and kept his word. I know that regardless of whatever desert he has in store for you, he will still keep his word. Even when you feel like you're free-falling, it is only a trick

of your perception. God holds you steady in
rest on that fact and know that all your effort
including your generative writing—are entir
his faithfulness. Yours is a gift springing from

A dear friend of mine lost his wife many years ago. When
I was in a period of suffering, he spoke out of his own experience and ministered to me in deep and unforgettable ways
by simply reciting a poem from heart. It is a poem by Minnie
Louise Haskins titled "God Knows" and I commend it to you as
a helpful reminder.

> And I said to the man who stood at the gate of the year:
> "Give me a light that I may tread safely into the
>   unknown."
> And he replied:
> "Go out into the darkness and put your hand into the
>   Hand of God.
> That shall be to you better than light and safer than a
>   known way."
> So I went forth, and finding the Hand of God, trod
>   gladly into the night.
> And He led me towards the hills and the breaking of
>   day in the lone East.
>
> *So heart be still:*
> *What need our little life*
> *Our human life to know,*

If God hath comprehension?
In all the dizzy strife
Of things both high and low,
God hideth His intention.

God knows. His will
Is best. The stretch of years
Which wind ahead, so dim
To our imperfect vision,
Are clear to God. Our fears
Are premature; In Him,
All time hath full provision.

Then rest: until
God moves to lift the veil
From our impatient eyes,
When, as the sweeter features
Of Life's stern face we hail,
Fair beyond all surmise
God's thought around His creatures
Our mind shall fill.

BENEDICTION

May you learn to take God's hand while you're still young. May he lead you toward the breaking of day in the lone east. May you embrace the story—every valley, every mountain.

HANDLING CRITICISM

*"To every reproach I know now but one answer, namely, to go
again to my own work."*
                                        —Ralph Waldo Emerson

For some strange reason the voices in my head clambered louder
than usual that morning. They had become more than voices.
Now they were actual people sitting on my desk and leaning
over my chair, rendering my efforts useless.

"Look, hurling metaphors like that doesn't make you a
writer," one would suggest.

Another would chime in with, "You're like the beef jerky of
literary talent, pal."

Still another: "So this is you trying to wear big boy pants
now? Cute."

Others were less cutting in their remarks, but equally
vigorous about the quality of my work or its truthfulness.

Each voice belonged to someone whom I admired, whether dead or alive, mentors who played a significant role in my life story, so you can understand why I squirmed in my seat. As I wrote, all their love for me had somehow translated into judgment. Their ceaseless commentary was imagined, but crippling: "Is this really what God thinks? Who are you to know? I mean, you and I both know that you're open to charges of hypocrisy, right? And when will you stop wasting your time on writing? There are so many other hobbies from which to choose, so many profitable things to do."

In a sudden moment of heated frustration, I looked each one of them in the eye as they sat in imagined spots around my desk and I said: "I love you very much and I'm really grateful for your impact on my life, but I can't do my job faithfully with you yacking in my ear. You'll have to go." I then shoved that person through the window above my desk—metaphorically, of course. Some were bigger than others and their imagined falls were more spectacular.

After they had all been tossed, I sat there shocked and a bit ashamed for a moment, but with the voices gone, I took the opportunity to start writing again before they returned. Two hours later, completely exhausted, I stopped. I reread the pages I had written and knew, deep down in my bones, that they were the best of my life. Something inside me jumped for joy and started declaring my liberation from the mental critics, but the next morning they were back. They had climbed up through the window and awaited my return, so I pushed them back out, saying, "I love you, but you'll have to go."

Once again, I wrote maniacally, but when they peeked over the windowsill and started whispering, I visualized shoving them back. Ironically, it's the writing I did after pushing those respected advisors aside that would please them the most. They do not know that, of course, and I do not plan on telling them, but I'm telling you because you, too, will suffer from the same well-intentioned desire to please your mentors. Writers need mentors, but your relationship to them holds an interesting tension—when to take their counsel and when to choose your own path. Sometimes their voices will wisely caution you and you should listen, but there may come a point when their advice is debilitating and you must throw them aside so that you can write according to the dictates that God gives to you.

OPENING OURSELVES TO CRITIQUE

The temptation to plug your ears to all criticism is great. But don't do it. Feedback from others can sharpen your writing skills and target your efforts more effectively. It can clarify your thoughts. It can help eliminate wasted movement. Imagine a basketball player who never took critique for his shooting form. He might eventually learn many things the hard way, but his shooting form would suffer. He would be far more effective with a little coaching. If that is true for sports, how much more so for something like writing? Call it what you want—coaching, criticism, mentoring—it is absolutely essential to faithful life-long writing. I will go so far as to say that effective generational, inspirational, and generous work *requires* good mentoring.

Nevertheless, we avoid critique. Why? Perhaps we fear it will tear away our carefully crafted masks. Maybe we suspect it will undercut our self-worth or lovability. I would like you to consider the possibility that by closing yourself off to critique, you're missing out on some of the things you want most. Don't you want to get better as a writer? Don't you want to be less agitated by other people's opinions. Don't you want to be less self-conscious, less self-absorbed. Don't you want to live free? You can only attain these things by freely exposing yourself to feedback, by growing accustomed to it, by letting your pride get used to the sting. How easily we rob ourselves of the freedom and gladness that accompanies self-forgetfulness, a sense of the work's value over and above one's sense of self.

In an eager effort to feel good about themselves, some people pursue feedback from those who only praise. They forget that too much praise dulls the wits. They forget to be people whose quality of work matters more than praise or criticism. It is all too tempting to listen to those who tell you what you want to hear. I know that criticism hurts, but it hurts less when encouragement is not your driving aim. Quality work that faithfully reflects the goodness, truth, and beauty of God is the driving aim of your efforts.

Let the right feedback from the right people direct your steps. Criticism from a lesser writer is unreliable, rarely useful, and you should rightly suspect feedback from a writer of unknown worth. Whom do you respect? To trust criticism, it must come from the mind of a trusted person, demonstrably skilled in the craft, who has the good of your work in mind.

LISTENING WELL

Never forget, either, that God likes to deliver wisdom and counsel from the most unlikely of sources, sometimes even from people who have nothing but your harm as their aim.

I once asked your grandfather how he handled all the criticism he encountered over the years as a physician. He reminded me of David's encounter with Shimei, the drunk, in 2 Samuel 16. Shimei, a member of Saul's extended family, met David just outside Bahurim. He approached David cursing and chucking stones. Abishai, one of David's mighty warriors asked for permission to decapitate the drunk who was, after all, insulting God's anointed one. But David settled him down.

"Let him curse," David said, "for God has told him to curse. Maybe God will use his cursing for good in my life."

The difference between the two warriors is striking. Abishai believed unjust accusations deserved harsh rebuke. But David entrusted himself to God even when attacked. David recognized what Abishai did not, that God's sovereignty over all things means that nothing comes our way by accident. Sometimes God sends us the message we most need to hear through the most unlikely of sources. David knew that something valuable and important might hide among all the vitriol and stone-throwing. A king, a physician, and a writer all need the truth that comes with criticism if they are to do their jobs well. Listen, therefore, but listen wisely.

CHANGE WHAT NEEDS CHANGING

Let's be honest. We're our own worst critics most of the time. We don't need any help being told we aren't good enough to make the cut. Indecision and spiritual torpor often come to those who listen to the accusatory voice in their heads. The voice typically points out the obvious: you lack talent, wisdom, insightfulness, creativity, and a dynamic personality. I encourage you not to engage that voice in debate. You will lose. And that voice is usually correct, in part. All you can do is keep working, reminding yourself that God likes to use little people for his kingdom work. You have plenty of shortcomings. So be it.

Unfortunately, we tend to be most critical about things that need our patience while failing to be critical enough about things we can and should change. I would rather be critical about the mole on my face, for example, than about my messy room. Or I try to change my personality rather than deal with a habit of lying. Or I criticize my writing style rather than fix my punctuation. I prefer vague irresponsibility to concrete responsibility.

Some things are fixable and others are not. Some things are morally right and some things are morally wrong. Some things are done well and some things are done poorly. Instead of repenting where we need to repent or changing what we should change, we tend to avoid responsibility. Writers cannot afford to avoid responsibility. Be eager to change what needs to change. Critique offers you opportunities to identify what should change and improve your work.

If you feel easily discouraged by criticism, remind yourself that what matters most is the final product, not your ego. Your job is to serve the work. Helpful criticism is an opportunity to refine what the Holy Spirit gave you to steward, to send it into the world in its best and truest form. Accepting critique in this manner requires humility. Step out of the way.

Quality work is typically the happy synthesis of your instincts contending with other people's instincts, your training colliding with other people's training until the work shines. In the end, the work is not wholly your own. Each time you finish a piece, stand at the threshold of the mystery of creation, hushed by the realization that the work has transcended your meager self, becoming something radiant to which you can have little claim. It's in that communion of ideas and creativity that the Holy Spirit loves to act.

BENEDICTION

May you be strong enough to embrace critique and wise enough to find worthy feedback. May your aim be quality and not adulation. May you ground your hope and your actions on the God whom you love, faithfully serving and stewarding the work he has inspired in you. Gladly embrace the mystery of creativity found in the communion of ideas.

THE ARCHITECTURE OF GOOD WRITING

"Am I a falcon, a storm, or a great song?"
—Rainer Maria Rilke, *Book of Hours*

I remember the pounding rain on the tin roof of my childhood home and the glass-paned front door through which we watched hail storms. I remember the concrete floor, the narrow hallway, and the three small rooms. I remember the kitchen window overlooking my mother's garden. And I remember the pantry where the candy jar sat on the top shelf.

We lived in a tiny house, and its architecture formed me. To this day, I love concrete floors. I still love narrow spaces and hammering rain on corrugated roofing. We build shelters and those shelters shape us. That's what architecture does. What we build—its design and its location—matters.

THE BASICS OF GOOD ARCHITECTURE

Good architects look at a project from many different angles before breaking ground. They care about easily-overlooked details—location, terrain, form, unity, light, materials. They care about what the structure will look like, what it will feel like, how it will amplify or mute sound. In the long run, everything matters.

As with building, so with writing. The architecture of your written work, like the architecture of a building, is a space into which others walk and are thereby shaped. Presentation matters. Pace matters. The details of your work shape others in mysterious and powerful ways. Generative writers thoughtfully consider these things and make adjustments as necessary. Are you being intentional about your work's architecture?

Nowhere is this intentionality more evident than when it comes to editing and refining your work. An experienced artist or writer knows that what you cut is as important as what you keep. Someone once said that books are not so much written as rewritten. In other words, eliminate the waste in favor of precision, even if it means killing your favorite paragraphs, an interesting word, or that clever turn-of-phrase. Sir Arthur Quiller-Couch famously said, "Murder your darlings." Don't be shy with the editing process. Remember the architectural principles.

My friend Dr. David Wang, author of *Architecture and Sacrament*, shared with me that architects evaluate a building's quality by seven attributes: coherent form, clear structure, compositional richness, grace, external and internal unity, historicity, and relationship to setting. Each of those attributes naturally overlap with writing and help us evaluate our work and write more effectively.

COHERENT FORM

In architecture, the parts of the building work organically to create a balanced whole. Do the parts of your work—the paragraphs and chapters—work organically to create a balanced whole?

The human heart is restless, the mind often impatient. We would rather rush to production than painstakingly attend to the details that make writing feel complete. Quite often, writers think they have created a unified work, but other readers find it difficult to follow. How does this happen? I think there are several possible answers to that question: some writers struggle with linear thinking, some are impatient, and others are simply unaccustomed to the demands of writing well.

I've tried to overcome my own weaknesses in this area by having a handful of readers—no more than five or six—who read my work before it gets published. They are a diverse group, each with a particular editorial bent. One has a good eye for overall flow, one improves my content by offering insights of her own, another is good at finding inconsistencies or gaps in my reasoning, still another has a strong eye for spelling and punctuation. Each one brings a unique gift. The overall result is a much stronger work.

CLEAR STRUCTURE

In architecture, the building is clearly and carefully organized. From the floor plan to the plumbing, the building is thoughtfully structured. Is your work clearly organized? Does it move smoothly and purposefully from beginning to end? Do the paragraphs naturally build upon each other? Does each sentence naturally follow the last?

We cannot write effectively without making some choices about what we want to say. Good writing is intentional. The decisions we make while planning are informed by macro and micro aspects of the writing process. You should always know where you're going in a particular piece of writing, and that can mean several things.

Do you have a beginning, middle, and end? Don't neglect the obvious. Have you decided each step along the way? I used to tell my writing students to pretend they are building a staircase for their reader. Make sure that there is no step missing, otherwise your reader will fall through and get hurt. Or, to change the metaphor, I tell them to lead their reader like Elliott leads E. T. in the movie *E. T. the Extra-Terrestrial*, using carefully-placed candy pieces. Eliott has to make sure that they are just the right distance apart to keep E. T. happily eating and following the trail. Writers need to treat their readers the same way. If you take care of them and lead them well, they will happily follow.

On a macro scale, do you know where you're going with your canon of work? Do your readers know what to expect when they pick up one of your books? Some suggest that you stick to one particular genre so that your readers know what to expect. That advice is fine in principle, but what if you want to try your hand at several genres? I've published memoir, poetry, and children's fiction. My work's continuity has nothing to do with genre, but they share a similar fingerprint, a similar tone and vulnerability. They share a similar vision. I want you to feel a similar freedom without sacrificing clarity or continuity.

COMPOSITIONAL RICHNESS

In architecture, the building is interesting without appearing pretentious. It feels natural and yet somehow beautiful. Is your writing richly layered without posturing? Does it feel natural to who you are?

And this attribute goes back to my earlier letter on being a conduit of life. The richness of your writing reflects who you are and there is simply no way around that fact. To play on the words of Jesus, a writer's heart brings forth the treasure hidden therein, for out of the abundance of the heart the pen speaks. Your written work can only be as rich as your heart and mind.

Attend to the layers and textures of your heart and your writing. When it comes to your fiction, ask yourself whether your characters are three-dimensional and complex. Do they feel real or do they feel wooden? Is your story an over-complicated plot or is it rich with human drama? When it comes to essays, ask yourself whether your arguments are simple or just simplistic. Simple is good, simplistic is not. Ask whether your insights carry a needed depth and truthfulness that matches the scriptures. Are you just trying to be clever? Is your poem trite? Careful readers instinctively recognize posturing. They recognize a lack of insightfulness and texture.

GRACE

In architecture, a building has more than a utilitarian purpose. Ideally, those who see it and walk through its interior feel moved. Is your writing more than useful? Does it move the soul? Does it pulse with grace and beauty? Some Christians, raised to care more for truth than anything else, pay little heed to beauty. Their work is helpful, but not lovely. Many Christians, however, are leading the charge for lasting and beautiful work. Their work sings, whether literally or metaphorically, because they are great lovers of God and what he has made. As Augustine said, "only he who loves can sing." I would have your work sing. Find those who are making beautifully and imitate them.

Although I risk making too short a list, here are some relatively contemporary Christian exemplars for you: For poets, look to Malcolm Guite, Dana Gioia, Scott Cairns, and Christian Wiman. For essayists, you can't go wrong with Thomas Howard, Makoto Fujimura, Marilynne Robinson. For novelists, read Leif Enger, Flannery O'Connor, and Walter Wangerin. These don't even begin to scratch the surface of the many Christians who have made beautiful work over the previous centuries.

You can be that kind of writer, moving us with the sheer beauty and grace of your work. Make our hearts beat to the pulse of grace. Sing us a new song.

EXTERNAL AND INTERNAL UNITY

In architecture, the building's exterior matches the building's interior. They share the same beauty and excellence. In your work, do the cover and content share the same beauty and excellence? Do they match?

In a pragmatic world, some care more about production and distribution than they care for the overall beauty of a book. If smaller fonts, tighter lines, and smaller margins can shave off a few pages and thereby save some money, so much the better. If the cover communicates the title and subtitle clearly with a nice stock photo, then job well done. Your primary job is to write, yes, but you should care about the final product in its entirety because you care about the reader's experience. You should care, for example, whether the font is easy on the eye, whether the page offers enough negative space around the words themselves to provide mental space for the reader, whether the font style fits the content, whether the cover reflects the content, whether the cover serves as its own worthy piece of art. Care about all of these aspects of the process, not just the content.

You will have to trust the book's design and illustration and typesetting to people who excel at making words lovely on the page, but be firm in your convictions. Challenge your publisher if their commitment to the aesthetic beauty of your work is not their priority. You will have to make compromises, yes, but do not abandon your words to mediocrity. Recognize that just as your gift is for putting words together, you will often have to trust in the gifts of others to make them beautiful as a book.

HISTORICITY

In architecture, the building occupies its place in history with dignity. Does your writing occupy its place in history with dignity? Does it converse with prior works published last year, five years ago, fifty years ago, five hundred years ago?

C. S. Lewis tried to read one old book for every contemporary one. He knew that we can get enamored with ourselves, duped into a chronological snobbery wherein we believe that those who came before us were a little parochial. We mistakenly think that ideas always evolve, that they progress. So we read all the latest on a given topic and forget that Plato or Augustine or Julian of Norwich touched on it long ago.

I met someone awhile back who liked saying, "It's 2020 now" or "We're well into the 21st century now," whenever she encountered a claim that seemed outdated. I'm prone to the same naivety. How quickly I forget that I'm confined to my time in history, that the prevailing errors are often my errors. My insights are more provincial than I know. My modes of thought are more insular than I realize. My writing can, therefore, feel untethered from any grand sense of historical conversation. To avoid such pitfalls, read widely, read across genres and across historical eras. Only then will your writing feel anchored in history.

RELATIONSHIP TO SETTING

In architecture, the building fits the natural terrain and texture of the land on which it is built. Does your writing feel natural to where you live, to where God has placed you geographically and historically? And does it harmonize with your life?

I'm a third culture kid, as they say, having grown up overseas. I'm a rural African at heart, but I spent my teenage years on a river in the Pacific Northwest, and now I live in urban America. So my writing has a little bit of all three coursing through it. These cultures have shaped me in significant ways and there is no reason to deny it. I'm a child of the plains and the Bitterroot Foothills. I feel most myself far from the crowd, far from the perpetual noise of city life. My writing no longer feels authentic to me or to my readers when I pretend otherwise. I cannot write like a Syrian refugee or a Russian tzar because I'm neither.

I'm also a creedal Christian, and that informs my character, my moral convictions, and my lines of thought. Because I'm a gentile, I'm an adopted child of Abraham, grafted into an ancient religion that teaches us to love God and love neighbor, to honor mother and father. God has given me parents by blood whom I must honor, but he has also gifted me with parents by faith. Honoring them with my writing prevents me from being overly concerned with sounding progressive. Does my work echo the sentiments of those saints who have written before me? Does it carry the same beautiful gravitas? I hope so.

THE PRESSURE TO BE UNIQUE

In architecture, some buildings are nothing but eye-catching anomalies designed by architects who believe that being unique is the primary creative virtue. You might be tempted to be like them in your writing. Or your teachers might inadvertently tempt you to be like them.

I was demotivated for many years by well-intentioned teachers who told me that the key to strong writing was a strong voice. They meant that I needed to find my particular style, to hone it so that it was unmistakably my own. What they said was true, but I thought they wanted me to be unique and the pressure got to me. Many young people feel a similar need to be unique in life. Let me alleviate you of that tremendous and unnecessary pressure right now, in writing as in life.

First, writers don't find their voice, it finds them after thousands of hours of writing. In other words, you will have to grow into who you are, your particular fingerprint. Don't go chasing your style, let it find you after many years of faithful writing. Given time, people will recognize your unique voice.

Second, your generative style, like your actual voice, will change over time. Age, illness, damage to the vocal chords, air quality, and life experience all shape the human voice. The human heart undergoes similar changes. Its expression in writing changes as a result.

Third, those who focus on finding their style flee imitation even though it is absolutely necessary for developing any skill in life. How can you write more faithfully and more generatively if you aren't imitating those who are better than you? The endless pursuit of individuality has wrecked many writers, so keep to sound architectural principles. The more architecturally sound your work, the more it will read like an act of grace and beauty unique to you, a somersault of the soul. Keep practicing without posing. Be silkworm, be flying fish, be oyster, wrote Kazantzakis. Bring forth beauty from your very deepest self and you may just astonish the world.

BENEDICTION

The nature of a tree incubates within the seed, waiting for its burgeoning. Likewise, the nature of your work incubates within you. Attend to it. Nourish it. Direct it. May your writing have a clear structure, compositional richness, grace, unity, historicity, and personal anchor. May it reflect the best parts of you in the best way possible.

SELF-DOUBT

"Our doubts are traitors,
and make us lose the good we oft might win,
by fearing to attempt."
    —William Shakespeare, "Measure for Measure"

I worked at a lumber store during one summer in college. Two buildings straddled the parking lot. The main store sat on the left and the wood storage barn sat on the right. The only way to get the wood from the barn to the delivery trucks was to drive a forklift *around* the parking lot.

On one memorable day, I was helping customers in the store when they suddenly froze. I followed their gaze and saw our youngest employee—a cocky high schooler—driving a load through the parking lot. He had stacked his lumber—about twenty 2x12x16 boards—on the forklift and jacked the forks as high as they would go so that he could clear the parked vehicles.

Now, the key to driving a wide load like that on a narrow fork-lift is twofold: keep the forks low and drive slowly. Because they were so high, he couldn't see the wood dancing all over the place while he carelessly drove at full speed.

He managed to cross the lot without dumping the load, but everyone watching stood terrified. His brainless swagger could have cost the company thousands of dollars in damages. And the shortcut *through* the parking lot was not worth the risk. He had plenty of moxie, but he lacked patience, common sense, and humility.

Writers need humility, too. Without it, they tend to careen into one of two unhealthy ditches: over-confidence or self-doubt. We either brandish our moxie or cower behind self-deprecation. This careening is not limited to writers. It's a human problem. It's a problem because we have a difficult time distinguishing between self-doubt and humility. Self-doubt is crippling; humility is life-giving.

BLIND SELF-DOUBT VS. INTELLIGENT SELF-DOUBT

Sometimes experience gives us an intelligent self-doubt that, in time, can serve us well. We learn, for example, to recognize where we go awry with certain lines of thought. We recognize our proclivity for unhealthy activities. We know our weaknesses. For example, I tend to biff it hard any time I try to skateboard or water ski or snow ski. That is a kind of *seeing* self-doubt and it is a gift from God. It provides wisdom that, in these cases, prevents injury. But this kind of self-doubt is not the doubt I address here. I've found that next to sin, *blind* self-doubt is the single greatest barrier to effective writing.

Blind self-doubt says, "I'm not smart enough, brave enough, interesting enough, dynamic enough, creative enough, or holy enough to write." What makes blind self-doubt so powerful is that we know these thoughts are somewhat true. That's why they so easily cripple our productivity and diminish our efforts.

This blind self-doubt is no gift from God, but a curse of vanity. It is the consequence of looking too long at one's self and one's perceived failures instead of looking at God. Faith looks to God, but this kind of doubt looks to self. Since faith is from God, not from man, your only chance to overcome doubt is found in looking away from self, looking toward God with your work and in prayer.

YOUR CALLING IS TO SERVE

You can't afford to let any thought-habits be a matter of secondary concern, especially as they concern the way you perceive yourself. Those perceptions define who you are, what you do, and what you become. Think rightly about yourself, therefore. Begin here: you're nothing more and nothing less than a servant in the house of God. Yes, Revelation 1:6 says we're kings and priests, but Jesus shows us how to be kings and priests: by serving. It's really that simple, and if you want to write generatively, you must keep it that simple.

Being a servant simplifies your mindset and gives you the opportunity to thrive in your writing. Like Anton Chekhov, you can "once and for all give up being worried about success and failures. Don't let that concern you. It's your duty to go on working steadily day by day, quite quietly, to be prepared for mistakes, which are inevitable, and for failures." Prepare yourself and set to work despite all the nagging questions and your history of failure. Serve.

Doubt may persist, but it is rarely helpful to get inside one's own feelings of self-doubt and analyze them. It only complicates matters. Therefore simplify. You are a servant. Effective servants focus outward, not inward. Self-doubt does the opposite. If you would be a ready and willing servant, combat the crippling effects of self-doubt by recalling to mind the convictions and principles that ward it away. Perhaps these convictions will engender courage and a right humility in you. Here are some principles that I've found to be helpful toward that end:

FIRST PRINCIPLE: PRAY

On the bookshelf near my writing desk, I have twin frames with two prayers. One prayer is by Dag Hammarskjöld, author of *Markings*: "Hallowed be thy name, not mine. Thy kingdom come, not mine. Thy will be done, not mine. Give us peace with thee, peace with men, peace with ourselves, and free us from all fear." The other prayer is an old Breton fisherman's prayer: "Lord, be good to me; thy sea is so wide and my boat is so small."

These two prayers remind me of who I am, who God is, and what I truly need from him.

When I stop praying these kinds of prayers, I gradually slide into an abyss. Before I'm aware of it, insecurity, fear, and shame have covered me, making it hard to breathe and nearly impossible to write. The more I pray dependently, the less I dwell upon my own insufficiencies and failures.

SECOND PRINCIPLE: PRACTICE COURAGE

Doubt is contagious, but so is courage. Courage is doing the right thing at the right time despite fear. Writing is the right thing to do when fear persists. You plant, and God will take care of the harvest (1 Cor. 3:6-7). In my experience, if you lift your eyes, look to God, and get to work, God loves to engender faith in your ability to accomplish the work through the work itself. Meaning, the more you write in faith, the more your courage grows.

C. S. Lewis said that if you want to be a courageous person then start acting courageously and you will one day wake up to find that you have, indeed, become courageous. Try doing the same thing with your writing. The facts are clear: you're not widely known, you do not write for thousands of adoring fans. In some respects, you can be thankful that you don't have to live with that pressure. Now is the time to build good habits that can sustain you if, or when, your work starts drawing a crowd. Write courageously now. Become dependable now. Live with integrity now and you will do so later. Carry yourself with the dignity and sincerity that God has called you to show to all people. Live faithfully and your writing will follow.

Faithfulness takes courage. It takes courage to stand by God's Word in a world that finds it outdated. It takes grit to vulnerably give yourself away in writing. It takes guts to plant trees while others are bulldozing them down. It takes an intrepid heart to get up and write every day. Who's going to read it anyway? And what if your work falls flat? That's why you should write for just a few specific people. You'll be surprised by your work's broad appeal if you target it to specific readers. At the start of each new writing project, I find it helpful to choose three specific people to whom I will write (Please note, these are not the same people I mentioned earlier who give critical feedback). They need to be people whom I know, but I don't tell them, I just keep them in mind. When I write for those three friends, my work remains targeted and vulnerable, my heart remains focused on them. My work is more concrete, more specific, and more people appreciate it.

THIRD PRINCIPLE: IMAGINE ABUNDANCE, NOT SCARCITY

I tend to notice limitations and obstacles rather than opportunities, and the result is that I make excuses. These reasons not to write compound my self-doubt, making me lethargic and subconsciously ashamed. In my mind, I not only lack sufficient wisdom or strength, I also lack time and energy. These are debilitating, though frequent, thoughts. They erode my courage. But there are ways to counteract them. If you want to limit the effects of self-doubt, shift your imaginative outlook from scarcity—in terms of time, finances, energy, opportunity, and talent—to abundance. Instead of staring at your empty left hand, notice that your right hand needs a little help holding all of the gifts God has given. In other words, change where you are looking.

Become increasingly aware of the disparity between your perspective and God's. While God makes lavish promises and floods our lives with good things, we spend most of our time, effort, and emotional capital worrying about what we do not have. We go to bed worrying about our lack and wake up to that worry.

This mindset of scarcity is more influential than we realize. Scarcity has infiltrated our cultural mindset and invaded most of our conversations. Even when our cups overflow, we sense our lack, not our fullness. We're a dissatisfied and unbelieving people with a skewed perspective, but God is not defined by limitations, obstacles, or scarcity. He is a lavish God.

Psalm 23 paints a picture of abundance and expansiveness, not survival, utility, and scarcity. With God as shepherd, we lack no good thing. He leads and feeds. He comforts and guides. He restores and anoints. He blesses until our cups cannot hold the blessing. God is so good that the psalmist has no doubt that goodness and mercy will follow him his entire life. That is abundance, not scarcity.

Those who live under the assumption that God gives generously and continuously make room for their souls to grow. They recognize that their abilities, their ideas, their time, and their community are gifts from a generous God. They will count their blessings and find it hard to keep track of them, feeling overwhelmed with gratefulness. After all, the earth is the Lord's and everything in it (Ps. 24:1) and "all things are yours" (1 Cor. 3:21). It may seem unbelievable, but that means God has given you enough time, enough money, enough energy, enough opportunity, and enough talent to serve him in your writing. When it comes to these things, a writer's well seems shallow to us, but if we pour it all out, we find that it is continually filled. Trusting in that continual fullness helps us learn the bottomless nature of God's provision and is one of the keys to becoming a mature writer. Act in faith even when your heart sees scarcity. God will come through in amazing ways and you'll develop the eyes of faith to see abundance everywhere.

FOURTH PRINCIPLE: PRACTICE GRATEFULNESS

The other day I heard about a global study finding that the happiest places on earth are filled with communities in which gratitude and service dominate over bitterness and selfishness. This "discovery" is old news to the Christian tradition. Our happiness has always depended upon gratitude articulated and verbalized—vertical gratitude to God and horizontal gratitude to our neighbor. Next to prayer, gratitude is our greatest weapon in spiritual warfare, and we should fight with it as Arthur fought with Excalibur.

Happiness is circumstantial, but thankfulness is not. Every time we give thanks, we acknowledge a gift that is out of our immediate control. Something is done for me by God, by someone else. I give thanks to that person for that thing.

People who never give thanks are often guilty of trying to control their circumstances. Manipulation, maneuvering, finagling become their *modus operandi*. In the end, they cannot hope in anyone but themselves. Those who stay vulnerable to the moment, however, and grateful for it can hope in the God who made them and placed them.

Thankful writers rarely try to control their circumstances or their success. They willingly trust the Lord as he equips them to write and as he unfolds their story. They can hope because God is in charge. They can hope because their failures or self-doubt have no bearing upon the faithfulness of God.

FIFTH PRINCIPLE: RECOGNIZE YOUR GIFTS

Socrates said that the highest end of a person's life was to know himself. He was only partially correct; the end goal of life is to love God and thereby come to a knowledge of one's self. This knowledge of one's self is essential to humility, for Paul sent a charge "to everyone who is among you, not to think of himself more highly than he ought to think, but to think soberly, as God has dealt to each one a measure of faith" (Rom. 12:3).

While he encouraged us to have the humility to think others better (Phil. 2:3), nowhere does he even imply that we should have a debased view of ourselves, certainly not of the gifts God has given to us. People who swagger or berate themselves are typically the two poles on the same continuum of vanity. They do not know themselves as they ought. True humility bows the inner knee to God. It recognizes that God gives the gifts we have, so there's no place for pride. It recognizes that God is at work, inviting us to use our gifts and work with him.

Because God labors, the humble labor too. Pride dreams about success and honor; humility gets down to work. In the writing world, people who want to be writers rarely want to do the actual labor of writing. They would rather dream vaingloriously of giving their Pulitzer prize-winning speech. What they want is not so much to write as to have written, to see their name on the cover of a book. True humility, on the other hand, just gets down to work.

LASTING CONFIDENCE

Do you feel unqualified and unaccomplished? Do you lack credibility? Is your pedigree poor? Is your network of connections feeble? Do you feel like a penny posing as a silver dollar? Have you done something you regret and hope that fame does not bring it to light? Whatever the source of your insecurities, you have two choices: either fix your eyes on the shame and allow it to plant doubt in your hope and creativity and vision, or fix your eyes on God and the work to be done.

Writers obviously need confidence if their efforts are to be sustained. Self-confidence is fragile, so where does confidence come from? Lasting confidence is the product of faith properly directed. If confidence is based on talent and on the reinforcing praise received, then confidence will take a hit more often than not. If confidence is in God's faithfulness to equip and strengthen, however, then a person's confidence is well-founded.

Write for the delight of the work. Write as an act of service knowing that your life depends upon serving God.

BENEDICTION

Cennini once gave this stirring call to artists: "You, therefore, who with lofty spirit are fired with this ambition, and are about to enter the profession, begin by decking yourselves with this attire: enthusiasm, reverence, obedience, and constancy." May you always work joyfully, soberly, obediently, and courageously. May you conquer self-doubt by trusting in the God who made you and placed you. May you grow confident by getting down to work.

BENEDICTION

"We see the brightness of a new page where everything yet can happen."
—Rainer Maria Rilke, *Book of Hours: Love Poems to God*

I begin this final chapter in the half-light, listening to the birds awakening with the sun. Christians all over the world awoke this morning, Good Friday, to remember Christ's death. But this morning I'm thinking of my grandmother, your great-grandmother. I called her Nana. She died a few hours ago, wrapped in a purple blanket we gave her. Although we have expected her graduation from this life to the next for some time now, I know this news breaks your heart. Death always feels surprising when it arrives.

For the past few days, Nana kept listening to old hymns and psalms that you and your entire school recorded back when you were in ninth grade. I recall the difficulty of coordinating that many people and that much equipment when we recorded. Students and staff of all ages had to rehearse for months. During the session, you all had to sing the songs several times to get them correct. So much practice and frustration went into that recording, but it was never released into the mainstream music market.

Probably only a few hundred copies still float around somewhere. All that work, for what? I don't presume to know all the results of that artistic endeavor, but I do know one. It escorted a dear saint from this life to the next one. Your voices and your songs sent her on her way. Your labor of love became a kind of benediction to her.

A benediction is simply the gifting of a blessing. One of my favorite benedictions comes from Numbers 6:24-26:

> "The Lord bless you and keep you;
> The Lord make His face shine upon you,
> And be gracious to you;
> The Lord lift up His countenance upon you,
> And give you peace."

You did not know it, but as Nana lay dying, you and your classmates were singing over her a benediction. It occurs to me this morning that there is a lesson here for you as a writer. All your months of work, hours of painful prayer, thankless service, and late-night labor may someday bless someone in ways you cannot predict. Your writing may escort them on a journey you will never know. For those who have not encountered Jehovah, your writing will point the way. For those who know and love him, your writing will be a benediction. Your words will spring to their minds at a hospital bedside. In an airport terminal. During a sleepless night. Alone on a mountain. Afraid in the dark. *Benediction*.

God said to Abraham, "In your seed all the nations of the earth shall be blessed, because you have obeyed My voice" (Gen. 22:18). The Gospel is the fulfillment of that promise and generative people—writers like you—are an essential part of bringing to realization God's promise to bless humanity. What a worthy call, evoking in us a new determination and patience!

PRACTICE BENEDICTION

None of your determination and patient work is wasted. All of it will somehow bless. Your work's purpose, like your life's purpose, is *benediction*. To all peoples, all tribes, all tongues, and all generations.

Easter reminds us that resurrection follows death. And Christ's resurrection is the ultimate expression of generativity. His aliveness is proof that the Lord has blessed us. He keeps us. His face shines upon us even now. We have his peace. So take heart. All of these chapters are resurrection letters. They are reminders of the magnificent calling to imitate him, point to him, pursue him, proclaim him. You're an extension of Christ. He is the fire. Your life is a lantern framing his flame.

Give me your hand. Let us consider two great paintings worthy of contemplation. Both paintings depict generativity and help cast a vision for the writer who hopes to live a long and meaningful life. The first painting is "The Lantern Bearers" by Maxfield Parrish. The second painting is "The Midnight Ride of Paul Revere" by Grant Wood.

"THE LANTERN BEARERS" BY MAXFIELD PARRISH

Do you remember summer nights in our back yard? We sat around the fire on worn, foldout chairs and read by the light of an oil lamp. You took it for granted that the lamp would work when we lit it, but what you didn't see was the work I put in to trim the wick, add clean oil, and clean off the glass. What mattered to you was the friendly light, not so much the lantern. In the same way, you attend to the details of creative work so that it effectively shines the light inside of it. God is the flame. Your work is his lantern.

In the painting by Parrish, we see the lovely result of lanterns carefully crafted to cast light beautifully. Attention has been given to the shape of the lanterns, to the tint of the glass, to the trim and accessories. Everything is chosen to enhance the light. In one respect, the flame matters more than the lantern, but it's the lantern's beauty that draws our attention to the light. Whatever you write, let it not only carry God's fire, but also cast his light beautifully.

The painting also highlights a communal aspect to creativity. The scene's beauty depends upon multiple people sharing the load and sharing the light. No doubt the painting

would still be beautiful with just lanterns hanging in trees, but it's the people that add character and dimension. Notice, also, that they are attending to more than their own lantern. They are helping each other because the more lanterns they hang, the more light they shed. It's as if they're sharing gifts with each other. Notice the expression of each lamplighter, the kindness of their gestures, the hope they inspire in each other, and the way all the faces are highlighted by those lighted globes. Notice the varied ages and the relaxed fashion with which they go about their labor. Nothing is forced, nothing self-centered. Their lights are not garish nor simply pragmatic. A lavish beauty and glad generosity infuse this painting. The entire scene cries, "Gift!"

Like them, you can attend to the craftsmanship of your lantern. Like them, you can create in community. Like them, you can go about your work without the pent-up anxieties of self-promotion that accompany the slavish mentality of this work-a-day world. Like them, your life and work are gifts. This is my deep hope for you, daughter, that you would wake up each morning remembering your God and walking with him in humble thankfulness. May your writing be an extension of his creativity, bearing his light in your life and in your writing as a gift given gladly to the world, a testimony to gratuitous beauty and divine generosity. You're a lantern bearer.

"THE MIDNIGHT RIDE OF PAUL REVERE" BY GRANT WOOD

Let us now consider the second painting. In Wood's imaginative depiction of Paul Revere, notice the winding road crawling out of dark woods. Notice the painting's muted tones and dark colors. Notice the proportions of the buildings and the people. They are recognizable but the proportions of the buildings and the people's faces seem surreal, as if this is more than just another small town and a handful of people and a horseman galloping. The entire road glows with an otherworldly light and the little town seems oddly spotlighted in a dark night. The world is shrouded in darkness except where Revere rides.

Although his horse's hooves hardly touch the ground, his efforts have only awakened a handful of townsfolk. His words and his urgency plunge them into conversation and, as we know by history, into action. The church dominates the scene with a spire spearing the dark sky and off in the distance, far behind Revere, we can glimpse some murky figures in the shadows. They are the enemy inevitably coming, and soon. In his trail, Revere's passionate ride leaves lighted windows and a people moved.

Great writing—like this painting—exudes an other-worldliness, the work vividly casting large shadows, the entirety of it drawing the eye of the heart to lasting things. The church looms large. Human passion, bewilderment, hope, and desires stand center-stage.

But much more can be learned from what Woods depicts. Like Revere, writers have a call they cannot deny. Like him, we must choose our actions deliberately and ride with a divine

urgency and purpose. Like him, we awaken a people to conversation and to actions that will have generational and cultural impact. Stand still and listen to the church bell ringing in a world largely shrouded, strangely lit. Listen to the whispers of the elderly and the running feet of children who hear and believe. Let the scene inspire you to life, light, and faithfulness. Trust that your simple, essential work as a messenger will be timely for many people, like a voice crying out in the wilderness, paving the way for the Lord.

Do you remember that wild-eyed prophet of old, John the Baptizer, living off locusts and honey? He, too, was poor. He, too, was misunderstood. Hear his words—simple, carefully chosen, and pregnant—springing up in the desert: "The One coming is greater. I'm lesser! He is the light. I'm only the lantern. He is the expression, the poem, the opinion and expectation of God dwelling among us, and when you see him you see the face of God!" This was John's anthem, the refrain of his life's song: hear him, follow him, imitate him. Like John, you're sent by God and compelled by his spirit to sing the same song.

God is the flame. Your work is a lantern. Lift your lantern high so it casts its light far and wide. Like John, you're a humble messenger who bears witness to the light of God, "the true Light which gives light to every man coming into the world" (John 1:9). John paved the way for the Lord in the backwaters of the known world; you pave the way wherever you are. John baptized with water; you baptize with words. Rise up, daughter! Rise up!

Thomas à Kempis once wrote, "A man is raised up from the earth by two wings—simplicity and purity. There must be simplicity in his intention and purity in his desires. Simplicity leads to God, purity embraces and enjoys Him." Perhaps this is the hidden thread, the driving hope of these letters—that you would simplify your calling and purify your desires. May these two attributes characterize your entire life's journey, but especially in your writing. I long for you to be raised up. I long for your heart to remain simple while your desires yearn, flaming, for the presence of God.

Hold on to God's promise to inspire and strengthen you. He gives power when you need it. He gives ideas when you need them. When you wait on the Lord, he supplies your needs so that you can do what he has called you to do. He will give you the ideas, the experiences, the margin, and the drive to accomplish what you were made to accomplish. Yes, you're just one person, but he multiplies your loaves and fish.

Keep working with your eyes open and your ears attentive to God's whispered voice. Learn to attend as much as your Father in Heaven attends. He speaks to us more than we speak to him, he calls to us more than we call to him, he rejoices over us more than we rejoice in him, he is more interested in our endeavors than we are, and he cherishes us as his poem. *Epiphany!*

THE FINAL BENEDICTION

Let us remind each other of these truths. Let us steady each other's steps. Let us spur each other on to more faithful work, deeper depths of insight, and higher hopes. We share the same calling and the same Lord. Let us wait upon him even as we work, even as we journey toward the city of God.

We're on the road that climbs God's holy mountain, the road which all his saints have walked. Up ahead, above the tree line, the city lights sparkle. Between here and there, we do not know what is in store. We do not know what we will accomplish along the way. This we do know—and in this knowledge we place great trust—that the One who began this work in us will bring it to completion (Phil. 1:6), that our life is being transfigured into his likeness day by day (2 Cor. 3:18), and that we will climb this mountain with our eyes fixed on Jesus Christ, the constellation of all our hopes and the source of deepest joy.

Get up into the high mountain, my child. You who bring good tidings to a broken world, lift up your voice. Say to us what we long to hear, "Behold your God!" Sing beautifully. Sing bravely. Unveil the heavens.

My daughter, child of God and my heart's song, imitate God who gave himself wholly to us, so that we might rise to life with him. Give yourself away so that others might rise to life with God. You're a diamond of inestimable worth, a star in the heavens of my heart. Your life already blesses many people and delights the One who made you. Continue loving what you see, loving what you do, and loving those whom you serve.

One night, I dreamt of a little girl who kept returning to the fire with arms extended and tiny hands cupped. She asked the fire for a white hot coal and the fire freely offered a piece of itself. She went away, and on her face was a fierce gladness and a riveted hope, evidence of a purified soul shining through her eyes. She returned again and again, with the same results.

My intrepid girl, keep seeking God. Keep carrying his light into the world!

The Lord bless you and hold you. His face shines upon you as he fills your life with grace. May you see his eyes gazing into your own. May you forever know his peace. *You are beloved.*

The time has come to close this book. The day is far spent and evening approaches. I hear a great cry in my heart to pull up my tent pegs and saddle my horse. I'm being compelled into mystery and unknown terrain where the mountain path climbs and the crisp air grows sharper. I hear the distant call of strange birds on high winds. They stir my expectations and invigorate each step. My God! I see a fire on the mountain, a common bush aflame among the steep crags. I'm coming, O Lord! Dragging this sluggish body by the will of my pen, approaching barefoot because this entire world is holy ground!

ACKNOWLEDGEMENTS

I owe an incredible debt of gratitude to Amy Kim, Judy Palpant, Pete Peterson, Kenton Spratt, and David Wang for poring over my manuscript with a magnifying glass. Making sense of my sentence fragments, expanding on my half-formed ideas, and ordering my scattered arguments is not a task for the faint of heart. Thank you!

To my students over twenty years of teaching, to The Oaks community, and to The Thinklings, thank you for helping me refine my convictions and for giving me the great honor of being a part of your joyous journey. May this book encourage you along the way.

To Shann Ray Ferch and Bruce Williams, thank you for spurring me on to write. You saw something in me and encouraged me to steward the gift. Thanks for pushing me gently and cheering me on.

To my wife and children, thank you for wrapping your arms around me and holding me up.

FURTHER READING

CHAPTER 1: THE MOUNTAIN BECKONS
Wind, Sand and Stars, by Antoine de Saint-Exupéry
Adorning the Dark, by Andrew Peterson
Art + Faith, by Makoto Fujimura

CHAPTER 2: THE WRITING LIFE
Culture Care, by Makoto Fujimura
Letters & Life, by Bret Lott
Letters to a Young Poet, by Rainer Maria Rilke
Culture Making, by Andy Crouch
For the Beauty of the Church, edited by W. David O. Taylor

CHAPTER 3: THE SANCTIFIED IMAGINATION
Ironies of Faith, by Anthony M. Esolen
You Are What You Love, by James K. A. Smith
A Grace Revealed, by Jerry Sittser
Chance or the Dance? by Thomas Howard
Surprised by Joy, by C. S. Lewis

CHAPTER 4: GRATUITOUS BEAUTY
Beauty Will Save The World, by Gregory Wolfe
Seeing the Form, by Hans Urs von Balthasar
Notes From The Tilt-A-Whirl, by N. D. Wilson
Awe, by Paul David Tripp

CHAPTER 5: THE CRAFTSMAN'S WAY
Mystery and Manners, by Flannery O'Connor
Second Thoughts, by François Mauriac
Wordsmithy, by Douglas Wilson
Zen in the Art of Writing, by Ray Bradbury

CHAPTER 6: LEARNING TO REST
Why We Sleep, by Matthew Walker, PhD
The Intellectual Life, by Antonin Sertillanges

CHAPTER 7: LISTEN
Book of Hours: Love Poems to God, by Rainer Maria Rilke
The Peregrine, by J. A. Baker
Wisdom of the Sands, by Antoine de Saint-Exupéry

CHAPTER 8: BALLAST
The Confessions, by St. Augustine
Systematic Theology, by John M. Frame
Simply Jesus, by N. T. Wright
Knowing God, by J. I. Packer

CHAPTER 9: CONDUITS OF LIFE
The Pursuit of God, by A. W Tozer
Mere Christianity, by C. S. Lewis

CHAPTER 10: CONTENTMENT AND AMBITION
The Whole Christ, by Sinclair Ferguson
The War of Art, by Steven Pressfield
A Long Obedience in the Same Direction, by Eugene Peterson

CHAPTER 11: TIME
Do More Better, by Tim Challies
The Screwtape Letters, by C. S. Lewis

CHAPTER 12: THE GIFT OF THE MUNDANE
A Theology of the Ordinary, by Julie Canlis
The Supper of the Lamb, by Robert Farrar Capon
Chance or the Dance, by Thomas Howard

CHAPTER 13: COMMUNITY AND SOLITUDE
Life Together, by Dietrich Bonhoeffer

CHAPTER 14: ANXIETY

Art and Fear, by David Bayles and Ted Orland

Guilt and Grace, by Paul Tournier

Gentle and Lowly, by Dane Ortlund

CHAPTER 15: SUFFERING

A Grief Observed, by C. S. Lewis

A Small Cup of Light, by Ben Palpant

A Grace Disguised, by Jerry Sittser

CHAPTER 16: HANDLING CRITICISM

Markings, by Dag Hammarskjöld

CHAPTER 17: THE ARCHITECTURE OF GOOD WRITING

On the Art of Writing, by Sir Arthur Quiller-Couch

How to Grow a Novel, by Sol Stein

On Writing, by Stephen King

CHAPTER 18: SELF-DOUBT

Walking on Water, by Madeleine L'Engle

Prayer, by O. Hallesby

CHAPTER 19: BENEDICTION

The Return of the Prodigal, by Henri Nouwen

Also from
RABBIT ROOM PRESS

BEATE NOT THE POORE DESK:
A WRITER TO YOUNG WRITERS
by Walter Wangerin, Jr.

SONGS FROM THE SILENT PASSAGE:
ESSAYS ON THE WORKS OF WALTER WANGERIN, JR.

THE DOOR ON HALF-BALD HILL
by Helena Sorensen

EVERY MOMENT HOLY
by Douglas Kaine McKelvey

RABBIT ROOM
— PRESS —